ALSO BY KEVIN NELSON

Baseball's Greatest Quotes

Baseball's Greatest Insults

The Greatest Stories Ever Told
(About Baseball)

Football's Greatest Insults

The Greatest Golf Shot Ever Made

Baseball's Even Greater Insults

Talkin' Trash: Basketball's Greatest Insults

Pickle, Pepper, and Tip-in, Too!

SLAP SHOTS

HOCKEY'S GREATEST INSULTS

Kevin Nelson

A FIRESIDE BOOK
Published by Simon & Schuster
New York   London   Toronto   Sydney   Tokyo   Singapore

FIRESIDE
Rockefeller Center
1230 Avenue of the Americas
New York, NY 10020

FIRESIDE and colophon are registered trademarks
of Simon & Schuster Inc.

Designed by Hyun Joo Kim

Manufactured in the United States of America

9   10   8

Library of Congress Cataloging-in-Publication Data

Nelson, Kevin, 1995.
    Slap shots : hockey's greatest insults / Kevin Nelson.
       p. cm.
    "A Fireside book."
    Includes index.
       1. Hockey—Quotations, maxims, etc.   2. Hockey—Anecdotes.
    I.   Title
    GV847.N36   1995
    796.962'02—dc20   95–18215
                                                          CIP

ISBN 0-684-81075-1

TABLE OF CONTENTS

PREFACE

Hockey is a tough game played by tough men. For all their fierceness on the ice, however, hockey players are a surprisingly modest bunch off it. This may have something to do with the nature of the game itself; it takes a lot out of a person to play hockey. You hit. You get hit. You skate. You chase the puck. You bang someone into the boards. Someone bangs you into the boards. You skate some more. Players are not inclined to strut around for the cameras after sixty minutes of that.

It may also have something to do with the Canadian personality. Despite the fact that hockey has become an international game, with worldwide appeal, it remains, first and foremost, Canada's game. And Canada tends to prefer, and cultivate, athletes who are somewhat less bombastic than the loud-talking, high-living, publicity-minded, endorsement-contracts-all-over-the-place athletes who reside in her neighbor to the south. The model for a hockey player is less Derek Sanderson and more Wayne Gretzky or Mario Lemieux, two superstars who make your typical Boy Scout look like a degenerate low-lifer wasting away in sin.

Nevertheless, there is great color in the sport of hockey. Great fun, great humor, great personalities. And, of course, great fights. I think we've captured a lot of that in this book, and I am confident that longtime hockey fans—as well as the millions of people who are just discovering the sport—will be entertained by it. The intent of *Slap Shots*, as with my other books, is simply to have fun—to poke fun at everybody I can without being mean-spirited, to have some laughs, to help hockey fans pass the time in a constructive way (that is, by reading about hockey) until the next game comes along.

I owe a great debt to many people for their contributions to this volume. They include: George Plimpton, Brian McFarlane, Jack Ludwig, Bruce Hood, Brad Park, D'Arcy Jenish, Stan Fischler, Gene Hart, Scott Young, Don Cherry, Dick Irvin, Trent Frayne, Chandler Sterling, Scott Ostler, Rick Reilly, William Houston, David Shoalts, and many more. I also want to thank my editor, Kara Leverte, for suggesting hockey as a sport with a treasure trove full of wonderful stories, an entertaining history, and fascinating personalities. She was right.

—Kevin Nelson

The more hockey changes, the more it remains the same: Keith Jones and Darius Kasparaitis brandish their "dangerous weapons" at each other. Photo by Marco Campanelli/Bruce Bennett Studios

1

A SHORT HISTORY OF HOCKEY

"These fellows have invented a game that is played on ice. They have fashioned knives which are fastened on their boots and they skate at each other in a menacing manner as they pursue a black rubber disc and propel it towards their opponent's wicket. There is a great noise and threatening as they advance toward the goal, brandishing their dangerous weapons at the enemy."

—Description by Englishman, late 1800s, on the newly invented game of ice hockey

"I went to the fights the other night and a hockey game broke out."

—Rodney Dangerfield, comedian and prototypical nineties guy

2

AND NOW, A LOOK AT THE GAME TODAY

Except for a Bobby Hull or a Bobby Orr, the NHL has always lacked for star power—marquee-type players who excite the interest of the casual fan just by the mention of their name. But that's changing. While Wayne Gretzky may not be a household name in the U. S. on the order of a Michael Jordan or Joe Montana, he is an authentic celebrity. And there are a host of other players—among them Mark Messier, Eric Lindros, Mario Lemieux, Pavel Bure, Patrick Roy, Doug Gilmour, Brett Hull—whose talents and personalities have made the NHL more popular than ever. Here is a look at some of the game's greatest stars today, as well as some of the less famous players:

A FEW LAUGHS WITH BRETT

You have to like Brett Hull. He is one of the biggest stars in hockey, and yet he has a wonderful sense of humor. He can make fun of himself, a rare trait among sports stars today. The fact that he blossomed relatively late as a hockey player and, of course, the fact that he is the son of one of the greatest players ever, seems to have given Brett an admirable perspective about himself and the game he plays so well. Here are some choice comments by Brett on life, hockey, and other important items:

On criticism that he shoots too much: "It's difficult to score without shooting the puck."

On being in shape: "Conditioning isn't the only thing that decides hockey games. If it was, the NHL would be scouting for players in YMCA classes."

On his first team, the Calgary Flames: "What bothered me about the Calgary Flames was their insistence on reducing hockey to a chin-up competition. If you could do a million push-ups, chin-ups and sit-ups, the Flames coaches believed you were a good player. They seemed to care more about physical prowess than offensive production."

On how much he sat on the bench in Calgary: "They could have made a bronze replica of my butt in a chair, and sent it to the Hall of Fame."

More about his lack of playing time for the Flames: "The only ice I saw consistently was in the bottom of my diet Coke glass."

On the charms of his college town, Duluth, Minnesota: "Even the climate is a lure: You freeze all that is dear to you in winter."

On coaches who ask one of their players to "shadow" scorers like Hull during a game: "My personal opinion on shadowing is that it's nuts. I believe coaches demean players by asking them to do it. If a coach wants a player to follow someone like he's a private detective, he should hire some high school kid."

On seeing longtime teammate Bernie Federko traded from the Blues: "Seeing Federko in a Red Wings uniform was unnatural, like hearing Neil Young doing a rap song."

On the investment advice he received from his mother: " 'Whatever you do,' she used to say to me, 'don't ever invest in anything that eats and poops.' "

FAT BRETT

Brett Hull—the glamorous, high-paid, good-looking hockey star—was fat as a kid. "At age seventeen," he recalls, "Wayne Gretzky and Mario Lemieux were headed for greatness. At age seventeen, I was headed for donuts." It's a charming and inspirational element of his life story—inspirational because many kids have weight problems and still want to play sports. Well, look at Brett Hull; *he* did it. Even as a minor leaguer, weight problems plagued him. "I was Vancouver's only right wing who came with love handles," he jokes. Though it must have been painful for him at times, Hull kept his sense of humor. He kept playing, and look what happened. "I got the perfect title for your book," a teammate told him once, *"From Fat to Fame: The Brett Hull Story."* And Brett was a big enough man to laugh.

THE HULL VS. CRISP FEUD

Youngsters may also find some reassurance from Brett Hull's experiences with one of his coaches when he was still trying to make it as a pro player. Not every coach is going to love and support you along the way; in Hull's case, one of them, Terry Crisp, could barely stand the sight of him. "I want you off my team," Crisp told Hull when Crisp was coaching and Hull playing for Calgary's minor league team. "I want you out of my town. I don't want you anywhere near my players. I don't even want you on my planet."

Crisp thought Hull was too lax, too easygoing. This was a common rap against Hull in those days, but Crisp took it to extremes. "Crisp rode me like he was trying to break a wild stallion," Hull recalls. "He wanted to break my spirit. He wanted to change my life and my playing style, simply because he didn't like them." Crisp, said Hull, tried to suck the creativity out of his game—for instance, by programming every pass on a breakaway. Hull thought this was ridiculous. "Once you get into that type of goal-scoring situation, the game becomes improvisational," says Hull. "I like to make it up as I go along." But Crisp didn't want that sort of spontaneous creativity, at least not from Hull, and the two quarreled.

Hull admired Crisp for his accomplishments as a player—he was a member of Philadelphia's two Stanley Cup–winning teams—and even liked him personally. But they clashed in their approaches to the game of hockey. Crisp thought Hull's tendency to put on pounds indicated a lack of seriousness. "Crisp often weighed my value as a hockey player by the numbers on the scale at weigh-ins," wrote Hull in his autobiography. "If I had put on a couple of pounds, he considered it further evidence I didn't care about hockey." Crisp, said Hull, "thought fear was a masterful coaching technique," comparing his reputation to that of a Stephen King horror story. After scoring 50 goals in a season in the minors, Hull came up to Calgary in the NHL, where Crisp had already arrived. It didn't matter where these two were, they just didn't get along. After Hull was named NHL Rookie of the Month in November, his coach benched him. "Hull is going in circles, rather than straight lines," Crisp told one reporter. This, after Hull had scored eight goals in twelve games.

Often the only solution for a troubled player-coach relationship is divorce, and that is what happened. Hull was traded to St. Louis in the spring of 1988, a change of scenery that proved a boon to his career. For the Blues he has assumed his father Bobby's legacy and become one of the NHL's leading goal scorers.

But he still looks back on the situation with Crisp and the Flames with dread. "What I learned in almost two seasons with Crisp was that I would never again play in a situation where the game stops being fun," said Brett. "If I ever find myself in another coach-player feud, then I'll either get traded or I'm quitting. You can't give me enough money to put up with that."

How Mario Saved Hockey (in Pittsburgh)

Until his back problems and his bout with Hodgkin's disease changed him and his game, Mario Lemieux of the Pittsburgh Penguins was a marvel, one of the best ever. "He could snap a puck through a refrigerator door," said Wayne Gretzky, exaggerating only a little. Another admirer, Trent Frayne, noted Mario's impressive size and likened his smooth skating to "a cruise ship docking." To be sure, it's a good thing Mario docked in Pittsburgh; otherwise it might be the Tampa Bay Penguins or the Saskatchewan Penguins. "Without him," explained a Penguin marketing director, "the team doesn't improve and the fans don't come out. He's meant everything to this organization." Oiler coach Glen Sather was more direct, as is his wont: "Without Lemieux, they pack up the team and move to another city."

With Lemieux, Steel City won back-to-back Stanley Cups. Like Wayne Gretzky, Mario was a teenage hockey phenom. Scouts realized early on that Mario was one of the chosen ones,

The great Mario Lemieux. "He could snap a puck through a refrigerator door."—*Wayne Gretzky.* Photo by Bruce Bennett

and Pittsburgh tabbed him No. 1 in the draft. "Anyone who'd miss Mario would miss Marilyn Monroe," said an older Pittsburgh scout with an eye for fifties-era sex symbols. Still, before the draft, a variety of NHL clubs whispered sweet nothings into Pittsburgh's ear, trying to lure the No. 1 pick—and the chance to get Mario—away from the club. Finally, Penguins GM Eddie Johnston declared what it would take for his club to deal that pick: "Up front, $1 million in a suitcase," he said. "Plus $200,000 a year for the rest of my life." Although maybe they should have, no teams took the bait, and Mario came on to write hockey history in Pittsburgh.

WHO WAS BETTER, MARIO OR WAYNE?

For a time it was a Mantle-versus-Mays debate, or, more appropriately, a Rocket Richard–versus–Gordie Howe debate. Who was the better all-around player, marvelous Mario Lemieux or wondrous Wayne Gretzky? Here are three informed opinions:

"On sheer ability, Mario is good enough to win scoring titles with a broken stick. On pure talent he's the best there is. But Wayne almost never disappoints you. He comes to work every night."
—Bobby Orr

"The comparison has gotten kind of tiring. I'm sure Wayne feels the same way about it as I do. We have fun pushing each other to be better but we want each to be known for just ourselves."
—Mario Lemieux

"You never lie awake nights worrying about who's better, because where does that get you?"
—Wayne Gretzky

Okay, okay, sorry we asked.

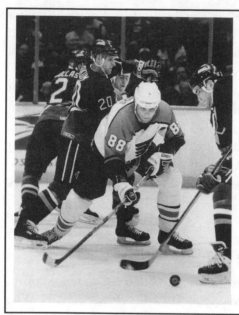

Eric Lindros mixes it up with Bob Corkum. "I don't claim to be an angel," says Lindros. "I get hit illegally and I do it back." Photo by Michael DiGirolamo/Bruce Bennett Studios

THE EDUCATION OF A HOCKEY PHENOM

Eric Lindros is another in a long line of teenage hockey phenoms that stretches back to Gordie Howe and beyond. When Lindros was a teenager they kept calling him "the next Gretzky," who himself was constantly being compared to another teenage hockey phenom, Bobby Orr. Lindros is in his twenties now and starring for the Philadelphia Flyers. Whether he becomes a player on the level of a Gretzky or Orr—or Mario Lemieux, another phenom— remains to be seen, but it's interesting to see what pressures he was under as a young man, before he even reached the NHL. Here, then, is a brief look at the ups and downs of a teenage hockey phenom:

On the Importance of Hockey as a Kid

"I never watched a lot of TV when I was a kid," says Lindros, "and I hardly ever read. It was just me and the rink." If you needed to find Eric, you looked for him at the rink. "Saturday is

God's gift to kids," he says. "I'd skip the cartoons and be out on the rink." When he was there, skating and playing and throwing his body around, he was in bliss. Eric even waxes poetic when he thinks about it: "Everything was so simple on the ice. It was just you, your stick, and a couple of pucks. The ice was crisp. My blades were sharp. The air was cool and bracing, but I felt warm. That was life."

On the Importance of Girls versus Hockey

For a teenage hockey phenom, girls rate below hockey. Just ask Eric: "Girls were pretty far down my list. When I was a kid I never saw Wayne Gretzky or Mark Messier hanging around with their girlfriends. If the stars of the game weren't hanging around with girls, I sure wasn't going to be caught hanging around with them."

On the Pressures of Junior Hockey

Though Eric loved the game, the pressures of junior hockey were pretty intense at times. In fact, because he was so talented, the fans may have picked on him more than other players. "Oh Gretzky, sit down!" they would yell after a mistake. His mother, Bonnie Lindros, talks about what it was like: "It's really hard to watch some of the things that go on in junior hockey. When 4,500 people are cheering because your kid has just been speared and is curled up on the ice in pain, it really hurts. Hockey can bring some people right down to the raw basics." Those raw basics included wisecracks about Bonnie herself. But her son learned to shrug them off. "My mom must be very, very busy, because I've lost count of the number of people who have told me they slept with her," jokes Eric.

On the Sault Ste. Marie Controversy

Lindros was drafted as a sixteen-year-old by Sault Ste. Marie of the Ontario Hockey League. This was, however, against his and his family's wishes. Eric did not want to play so far away from

home, and he refused to sign with the team. This created a huge
stink in which many Canadians accused Lindros of being a
spoiled brat who was trying to dictate where he was going to play.
For his part, Eric saw himself as a pawn being used by people
who didn't really care about his welfare. "The whole episode
showed me that hockey is a bottom-line business, even at the junior level," he recalls. "I felt like a piece of meat."

As he promised, Lindros did not play for Sault Ste. Marie,
which eventually traded him to the Oshawa Generals of the
OHL. After Lindros became a General and showed up at Soo
to play for the first time, the tension was so thick you could cut
it with a hockey stick. Sault Memorial Gardens hired police
guards to protect Lindros from the potentially unruly home
crowd. "It's kind of bizarre when you have to take those kinds
of safety measures at a junior hockey game because of fears that
some loon might get out of control," he says. "But I don't think
it really affected me. The way I viewed the situation, it was just
like having a whole bunch of baby-sitters there—and I wasn't
the baby." Years after the controversy, Sault Ste. Marie fans
remained bitter toward Lindros, but he wasn't having any
part of it. "Who needs that stuff?" he says. "Dump on me if you
have to, I made the decision. But the decision's made. Get a
life!"

On His Image as a Hockey Player

The Sault Ste. Marie controversy turned the teenage Lindros
into an ogre in the eyes of some fans. Eric's response to these critics is, as usual, to the point: "I'm not evil, I don't wear black. I'm
not the made-up, superficial jerk they're so proud to portray me
as in the papers." One reason why some people see Lindros as a
bad guy is the physical, body-banging way he plays hockey. "I
have to play a physical game, or I'm not into it," he explains. "I
have to bang somebody. I'm not some little freelancer who can
wheel and deal and not hit anyone."

On His Philosophy of Hockey

Lindros does not apologize for the way he plays hockey. "I don't claim to be an angel," he says. "I get sticked all the time, I get hit illegally, and I do it back." Not backing off from the challenge of an opponent in juniors, he rationalized it this way: "I almost got into a fight with Jeff Hardy. I figured, 'What's he going to do? Bash out my teeth?' My uncle Dan's a dentist. He can make me a new set." Adding, "That's what it's all about. Deck or be decked."

On the Player He Admires Most

Eric Lindros's role model as a youngster was not Gretzky or Lemieux, it was Mark Messier. "Watch Mark Messier when he loses a faceoff," said Lindros in awe. "He lays a beating on the guy right there at the draw. It's just the way he plays. Some people don't like it, but he wins the next faceoff. Job's done." Lindros admired Messier's imposing physical presence, his ability to win and to excel under pressure—and well, other things too. "Mark Messier was the big guy for me," says Lindros. "I was impressed by his physical presence and his leadership qualities—also his Porsche."

L'Affaire Québec

The Quebec Nordiques chose Lindros as the No. 1 player in the 1991 NHL draft. But, as with Sault Ste. Marie in the juniors, Lindros refused to play along. "I just don't feel the Nordiques care about winning," he explained at the time. "I can't be part of an organization where I don't sense that fierce commitment to be the best." As you might expect, the Nordiques were not thrilled by young Eric's pronouncement. "There is no bleeping way an eighteen-year-old is going to tell me what to do," said a furious Marcel Aubut, owner of the Nordiques. "We are taking off the gloves." They took off the gloves all right, but in Eric's case they were the hockey gloves. Feeling that he was again being jerked around by the hockey powers that be, Lindros would not sign with the Nordiques.

Thus began a standoff between the Lindros family and the owner of the Nordiques. Lindros refused to budge, so did Aubut, and an entire year passed. "I just couldn't play for an organization that treats people and does business like the Nordiques," said Lindros, adding, "the Nordiques haven't learned that players are people, not machines."

Finally, Aubut did trade the rights to Lindros at the following year's NHL draft. Caught up in the frenzy of bidders for Lindros, Aubut got carried away and decided to make deals with not one, but two NHL teams, the Philadelphia Flyers and New York Rangers. The NHL was forced to hire an arbitrator, who decided in favor of the Flyers.

In this fight at least, Eric did not wear the black hat; that fitted perfectly on Aubut's head. "The Lindros fiasco was created by Marcel Aubut, who has been doing this kind of negotiating for years," Edmonton coach Glen Sather charged. "It's time somebody stood up to him and told him to stick his negotiating where the sun doesn't shine. It's typical Marcel Aubut. He's trying to orchestrate and squeeze somebody to get another buck." Toronto columnist Christie Blatchford joined in. "It turns out in the protracted battle of wills between Quebec Nordiques owner Marcel Aubut and Eric Lindros *et famille*, the guy who behaved all along like the responsible adult was the teenager," Blatchford wrote. "It wasn't Lindros who agreed to a deal first with one club, then with another for more dough; it wasn't Lindros who tried to back out of the first deal. It was *Bébé* Aubut."

Two Opinions of Eric

"I really get the feeling that there are a lot of people who want to see me fail," said Eric Lindros. "I'm not exactly loved by everyone on the planet." That's for sure. No one seems to be lukewarm about Eric Lindros; every hockey fan seems to have an opinion about him, and they either love him or hate him. This was perfectly demonstrated at a Flyers game, in which a Philly fan held up this sign: ON THE EIGHTH DAY, GOD CREATED ERIC LINDROS.

A sportswriter, spotting the sign in the crowd, snarled, "If Eric Lindros is God, I want to go to hell."

TALKING HOCKEY

A tie, said Bear Bryant, is like kissing your sister. But Edmonton's Bruce MacGregor is against using shootouts as a means of breaking hockey ties at the end of a game. "I don't see NFL games being decided by somebody throwing a ball through a tire," he says. . . . The St. Louis Blues were on a losing streak and a reporter asked winger Kelly Chase if the team was beginning to feel the pressure. "Does a one-legged duck swim in a circle?" snapped Chase. Tell you the truth, Kelly, we haven't watched many one-legged ducks lately. Does it?

"It was like I got a free buzz and now I have the hangover," Sharks center Jamie Baker said after he collided with a teammate and knocked his head on the ice. . . . Irritated by Peter Stastny's poor play, New Jersey Devils coach Herb Brooks said that Stastny's $700,000-a-year contract was "the biggest heist since Brinks." Stastny wore a Lone Ranger mask to practice the next day. . . . Sportswriter Bill Tammeus jokes, "As fast as the sports world changes, it's reassuring to note that a sub-.500 record still can get you into the NHL playoffs."

After Blackhawks defenseman Chris Chelios received a fine for high-sticking Sergei Fedorov, Chelios blasted Fedorov and European hockey players in general. "Europeans always tend to lie down on the ice longer than anyone else. They're like soccer players," said Chelios. He added, referring to Fedorov: "He's a faker and a liar." . . . And a cheap-shot artist too? Fedorov's brutal cross-check of San Jose's Jayson More in a 1994 Stanley Cup

playoff game was "the most glaring example of a player trying to
do serious harm to another," said reporter Steve Kettmann.
Here's how More saw the incident: "From the time I hit him in
the corner, [Fedorov] cross-checked me five times. And they
weren't just cross-checks. He was trying to hurt me. It's lucky he
got me in the head, or I might be hurt."

After St. Louis Blues defenseman Robert Dirk popped in a
goal, only his second in five years, goalie Curtis Joseph cracked,
"Now that Dirk has all this offensive prowess, we'll have to find
a stay-at-home defenseman to play with him." . . . St. Louis GM
Ron Caron once called Blues star Brett Hull "a floater." Hull's
teammate Adam Oates responded, "I find it hard to believe that
a guy who scores 160 goals over two seasons can be called a
floater."

Over at the Quebec Nordiques, coach/GM Pierre Page assessed
his team's chances of making the playoffs one year this way: "No
chemistry, no hitting, no board contact, no back-checking, nobody
comes to play. We need three miracles, a little pride, and the other
teams not to win any more games." Those other teams failed to
comply, and the Nordiques dropped like a rock. . . . Kings coach
Barry Melrose correctly guessed that a ref would call a penalty
on one of his defensemen. "Maybe I'm clairvoyant," said Barry,
"or maybe I've been watching the Dionne Warwick channel."
Considering Barry is an up-and-coming media guy these days,
probably the latter. . . . And was Mario Lemieux ticked off, or
what? "I've done all I can," he told a reporter a couple of seasons
ago. "From now on, I'm not going to get involved with the league.
I'm not going to do any more promotional things. I'm done with
that kind of stuff. They can promote the marginal players if they
want." The definitely non-marginal Mario was fed up with NHL
officiating.

Hockey players' complaining about the officials is not new. But
things *are* changing in the NHL. Just ask *Sports Illustrated*.
"Gone is the image of the NHL player as a toothless face-buster,"

it said in a much-celebrated article, proclaiming pro hockey "a hot" sport. That's in contrast to the old days, when hockey was a "boil" on the professional sports scene and hockey fans, according to the magazine, "looked like the spillover from Wrestlemania." Oh yeah? Want to fight about it?

BE GRATEFUL, IT COULD HAVE BEEN THE MIGHTY *MICE*

The Anaheim Mighty Ducks is one of the NHL's newest and most successful franchises. Owned by the Disney Corporation, it is the only team in sport named after a movie, which, not coincidentally, was made by its parent company. Judging by Mighty Duck merchandise sales, fans seem to like the name, though it received considerable ridicule at first. Los Angeles columnist Mike Downey wrote new words to an old standard when he heard what Disney was going to call the team:

> "Now it's time to say good-bye
> To all our company,
> M-I-G (Gee, what a stupid name for a hockey team)
> H-T-Y (Why? Because we made a movie)
> D-U-C-K-S."

Toronto columnist Jim Proudfoot is not one of those mocking the team's name, however. "No matter what, we can't cast any stones at other nicknames," he writes. "After all, we have a hockey team [the Maple Leafs] that is a grammatical error." Then there is the testimony of a Los Angeles zoo curator who says that ducks are, in fact, pretty mighty creatures. "Ducks fiercely defend their territory," explains Mike Cunningham, whose specialty is birds. "Ducks stick together. And when two ducks fight, well, one duck will grab the other duck with his beak and hold him, then pummel him with his wings. That fits the hockey image, I suppose."

HOCKEY PLAYERS AND THEIR TEETH

Hockey players wear helmets to protect their head and mouth-
guards to protect their teeth. Still, they lose their teeth the way
some kids lose shoes. "I hid my linemate Robbie Pearson's false
teeth in his jar of hair gel once," says Eric Lindros, recalling a
practical joke he played on a teammate. "He wasn't too thrilled
with that, but he would always make sure to exact his revenge.
Whenever the team went for meals, you could usually count on
Robbie's false teeth ending up in someone else's glass before we
left the restaurant."

Next to an accountant and an agent, a dentist remains one of
the most important people in an NHL player's life. Though
Derek Sanderson, formerly of the Bruins, hated *his*. "I haven't
gone to have my teeth checked in fourteen years," he said when
he was still playing. "I had them drilled then. To me that drill is
a shattering experience. I keep thinking of chalk on the black-
board making a screeching noise. Ugh!" But Derek should feel
grateful; at least he had some teeth. "They were a curious gang
of Canadians who, as part of dressing for a game, took out their
teeth and put them in paper cups," wrote Bill Lyon, describing a
Philadelphia Flyers team of some years ago.

It's always been that way with hockey players, and maybe
always will be. Though some players may have found a way
around it: Don't hit so hard. There was such light hitting at a recent NHL All-Star Game, noted Phil Jackman, that "some of the
guys didn't even remove their dentures."

LOOKING FOR JUSTICE

Chicago Blackhawk goalie Ed Belfour smashed Calgary's Sandy
McCarthy across the jaw with a forearm in a 1994 game. But
Belfour received only a minor penalty, which incensed Flames
coach Dave King no end. He wanted to see Belfour ejected. King
was not going to send a videotape of the hit to the league office

to seek justice, however. "I'm sick of tapes," said King. "I'd rather see somebody beat him up."

THE CURSE IS DEAD

In winning the 1994 Stanley Cup, their first in fifty-four years, the New York Rangers did not just get the monkey off their backs, they got the dragon out of the basement. According to Ranger legend, a dragon lurked beneath Madison Square Garden, creating bad luck for the home team. Certainly the New Yorkers had their share of it over the years, beginning with the fabled curse of Red Dutton, who, after being put out of business by the Garden's team, declared, "The Rangers never will win the Cup again in my lifetime." Was the curse for real? Did Dutton really say that? "A lot of that was newspaper stuff," he said on his death bed a few years ago, "but newspapers can be right sometimes."

The Rangers finally laid Old Man Dutton's curse to rest, but it wasn't easy. Forget the previous fifty-three years, which were

Mark Messier was one of the "Men of Edmonton" imported to New York to break "the Curse" and bring the Rangers home a Stanley Cup title. He did. Photo by Bruce Bennett

tough enough. The 1994 playoffs were an endurance test in itself.
The Rangers needed huge helpings of skill, stamina, and, yes,
luck to win it all. They beat New Jersey in seven games in one of
the most thrilling playoff series ever, then moved on to face Vancouver in the finals. There was no getting away from the curse,
even then. After Vancouver goalie Kirk McLean stopped a million or so Ranger shots and the Canucks won Game 1 of the series, the headline of a Vancouver newspaper trumpeted THE JOY
OF HEX. And chants of "1940! 1940!"—the last Ranger championship—filled Pacific Coliseum when the series shifted to Vancouver.

The series against New Jersey was a marvel, one to preserve
in the time capsule. "Ask anybody in the game," said Devil defenseman Ken Daneyko. "The money's great, the accolades are
great, but all they want is their name on the Cup." That's all the
Rangers and the Devils wanted, and they put their bodies on the
line to prove it. Bernie Nicholls of New Jersey nearly cross-
checked Ranger forward Alexei Kovalev into oblivion. In the
locker room afterwards Michael Farber saw Kovalev up close:
"[He] looked as if he'd been in a train wreck." Rangers coach Mike
Keenan, who was soon to have plenty of troubles of his own, called
the hit "an act of violence," which Nicholls dismissed offhand.
"Mikie is doing a lot of talking over there," he said. "We're not
paying much attention." But Nicholls could not dismiss the NHL,
which suspended him for one game of the series.

Kevin Lowe of New York and Claude Lemieux of New Jersey
had themselves a little tiff too. Lowe claimed that in Game 2
Lemieux bit his finger—no, actually chewed on it, like a dog with
a bone. It reminded some of the time Lemieux practically swallowed one of Jim Peplinski's fingers. "Somewhere in his background," said New York's Craig MacTavish, "there must be a
rottweiler."

Meanwhile, the Rangers and Devils were going at one another
like cats and dogs. The Devils took a 3–2 lead in games, with the
sixth game to be played in New Jersey. This prompted Mark

Messier's now-famous prediction: "We know we are going to go in there and win Game 6 and bring it back to the Garden." In recent sports history, Messier's statement ranks with Dallas coach Jimmy Johnson's bold prediction that his Cowboys were going to wallop the San Francisco 49ers in the 1993 NFC Championship. Going back farther, it was also remindful of Muhammad Ali (then Cassius Clay) saying he was going to whip Sonny Liston for the 1964 heavyweight title, or Joe Namath's 1969 prediction of a Super Bowl victory against the Baltimore Colts. In each case, the man gave meaning to his words with action. So did Messier. He scored not one—not two—but three goals in the third period to almost singlehandedly bring his Ranger teammates back from the edge of the cliff where they were poised, Red Dutton's words ringing in their ears, ready to jump. "He leads and they follow," said an admiring Bernie Nicholls about the role of Messier on the Rangers. And they followed him back to the Garden for an it-doesn't-get-any-better-than-this (unless you're a Devils fan) double-overtime Game 7 win.

Messier's contributions throughout the series and the season were yet another sign of a front-office policy that had paid big dividends for the New York club. That policy—whether consciously pursued or not—can be summed up in two words: Get Oilers. After the Rangers did an El Foldo routine in the 1991 playoffs, a disgusted Neil Smith said, "The playoffs separate the men from the boys, and we found out we have a lot of boys in our dressing room." So what did the Rangers general manager do about it? He brought in men from Edmonton.

In September 1991 Smith signed Adam Graves, a former Edmonton Oiler who has since become "the NHL's most highly skilled bodyguard," in Austin Murphy's words. Then, a month later, Smith bagged Messier, one of the most famous ex-Oilers of all and a man with a fistful of Stanley Cup titles to his credit. Then Jeff Beukeboom arrived. The following season saw Kevin Lowe and Esa Tikkanen come over. Then, loading up for the 1994 spring playoff crunch, two aging veterans with Oiler bloodlines—

Craig MacTavish and Glenn Anderson—completed what came
to be known as "Edmonton East."

"Last year someone in the organization told me, 'Enough Oilers,' said Smith. "What should I get, then, Sharks and Senators?
I never went after Edmonton players by design. But these guys
became available and seemed to fit our needs. These are world-
class players. They've done things. God bless them if they want
to put on our uniform. They are guys who can lead you through
adversity."

In the finals against Vancouver the Rangers encountered adversity from an unexpected source—their coach. Hardly popular
with his players to begin with, Mike Keenan alienated practically
every Ranger fan who has ever existed, dead or alive, with some
of the most underhanded actions since the latest Tom Clancy
novel. When press reports surfaced that Keenan was engaged in
hot and heavy negotiations with the Detroit Red Wings to take
over as coach and general manager, Iron Mike stonewalled with
the skill of an Oliver North. "I am not going to Detroit," he said.
(That's true, Mike went to St. Louis.) "I signed a five-year contract when I came here. There is no escape clause," he said. (Nevertheless, Mike found one.) "My mission here is not to win the
Stanley Cup, but to win the Stanley Cup a number of times." (Just
not with the Rangers.)

The New York players tried not to be distracted by the flap
over Keenan. ("It's Mark's Mess Now" shouted the *Daily News*.)
They had long grown tired of their coach's act anyway. "Keenan
won't make one save, he won't score a single goal," said goalie
Glenn Healy, Mike Richter's backup. "It will be us players who
win or lose the whole shebang." Down three games to one to New
York, the Canucks looked dead and buried. But they beat the
Rangers in the Garden in the fifth game and beat the Rangers
again in the sixth game in the Pacific Coliseum to force a seventh
and final game in New York. Capping one of the best NHL playoff seasons ever, the Rangers did indeed hang on to win the whole
shebang.

New York went wild. "Madonna is so thrilled about the Rangers' winning the Stanley Cup that she promised every player on the team two minutes for high-sticking," joked David Letterman. Everyone but Madonna seemed to hold, touch, or drink from the Stanley Cup in the celebration that followed. The great thing about the Cup is that, unlike other sports, it's not some sterile object that is locked away in a trophy case for the unwashed masses to look at, but not touch. The unwashed masses can wash their hands in the Cup—and do just about anything else that will fit. Besides getting their names inscribed on it, the winners get to take the Cup home or wherever they choose. After the Ranger win, a horse ate from it, a baby sat in it, and on MTV they filled it with clams and oysters. At least one longtime NHL hand thought this was appalling. "The amount of disrespect shown it is mind-boggling," said Ole Peterson, whose family redesigned the Cup more than thirty years ago. "These jocks should not be behaving like jerks."

But even Ole could forgive the Rangers for their exuberance. "I don't blame the Rangers," he said. "They've waited fifty-four years." The wait was long, the wait was hard, but the dragon of Madison Square Garden was no more. "All the ghosts," said Mark Messier, the No. 1 dragon slayer. "All the bad luck for this organization. That's what made this one different. Nineteen-forty, rest in peace."

THE GREAT ONE

Wayne Gretzky is "the Man." Or at least he was. He's older now and not what he used to be. But then, as Dizzy Dean used to say, Who is? Though, in some ways, Gretzky will always be the Man. That will never change. Because even though his records may some day be eclipsed by some Gretzky of the future, it will be hard, if not impossible, to replace him in the hearts and minds of hockey fans. As others have pointed out, Gretzky wasn't just a hockey player; he *was* hockey. For some, such a responsibility might have proven an overwhelming burden, but for the Great One, as with all things seemingly in his charmed life, he handled it with grace and honor, light as a feather.

The Irritating Mr. Gretzky

You've got to hate guys like Wayne Gretzky—well, no, you've got to love Wayne, but you've got to hate guys *like* him. Because if Wayne Gretzky were anybody but Wayne Gretzky, he'd be really irritating. Listen to what these people have to say about him:

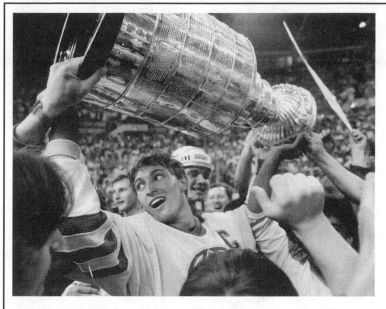

Wayne Gretzky hoisting the Stanley Cup in 1985. Says Gretzky: "I've
held women and babies and jewels and money, but nothing will ever feel
as good as holding that Cup." Photo by Bruce Bennett

*"He seems almost too good to be true. He is not merely the best
hockey player in the world, but one of the nicest and most un-
spoiled."*
—A writer

*"As approachable, intelligent, witty and articulate as any ath-
lete in pro sports."*
—Stephen Hanks, Gretzky biographer

*"His personal charm as well as his scoring feats have endeared
him to the North American public."*
—Canadian Encyclopedia

*"If the world's leading marketers got together to invent the ideal
athlete to endorse their products, anyone suggesting an athlete*

with the credentials and personality of Wayne Gretzky would be accused of pipe dreaming."
                                        —*Advertising Age*

"He is polite to the press, indulgent with his fans, gives generously to social causes, and voices no political opinions. His display of virtue and clean living ranks the Great One among the most remarkable entertainment professionals of this, or any other time."
                              —Joseph Romain and James Duplacey,
                                        more Gretzky biographers

Handsome, rich, modest, a credit to his community, a family man, a team player, has a beautiful wife, is the greatest hockey player ever—man, you are really getting on our nerves, Wayne!

MORE PRAISE OF WAYNE

Wayne Gretzky excites praise not only for his Boy Scout behavior off the ice, but, of course, for the marvelous things he does *on* it. Sportswriters and even rival players wax poetic when Gretzky starts doing the things that he, and only he, can do so well. A sampling of great lines about the Great One:

"Those two guys are talking without words."
                              —Flyer captain Dave Poulin, after
                              Gretzky and Oiler teammate Paul Coffey
                              dismantled Philly in a game

"He's so fluid, he'd slide through mesh."
                              —Opposing player, watching Gretzky
                              skate

"Gretzky makes me feel like an old man."
                              —Marcel Dionne, then twenty-nine, after
                              watching Gretzky the teenage wonder

"He was so great, we were able to follow on his coattails for years. In our hearts he's still part of this."

—Oiler defenseman Kevin Lowe, talking about Gretzky after Edmonton won the 1990 Stanley Cup without Gretzky

"Wayne Gretzky is almost impossible to check. The theory is, ride him off the puck. But how are you going to bodycheck him? The only way to do it is to hit him when he's standing still, singing the national anthem."

—Harry Sinden, Boston GM

"Some guys play hockey. Gretzky plays 40 mph chess."

—Lowell Cohn, sportswriter

"Intensity and concentration and desire. He can put these three together better than anybody I ever saw."

—Phil Esposito, who had plenty of those three qualities himself, on Gretzky

"Mathematically, if he had been hitting home runs, Gretzky would have thumped No. 97."

—Writer, making a baseball analogy after Gretzky got 163 assists in the 1985–86 season. The previous record holder was Bobby Orr with 102.

LISTENING TO WAYNE

"When Wayne Gretzky talks," said Ed Johnston, "everybody listens." Johnston said this during NHL strike negotiations a few years ago, and he was referring to the high esteem in which other hockey players hold Gretzky. Everybody in hockey does listen to Gretzky and although he can be, as one reporter said, "infuriatingly humble," here is what he has to say on a variety of topics:

On winning the Stanley Cup: "I've held women and babies and jewels and money, but nothing will ever feel as good as holding that Cup."

On the pursuit of excellence: "I hate mediocrity. If there's one thing I can't accept, it's mediocrity."

On winning the Lady Byng Trophy for sportsmanship: "Some guys might rather win a case of lipstick."

On his playing style: "I don't go banging in the corners. The way I see it, corners are for bus stops and stamps."

On breaking the records of Gordie Howe, Bobby Orr, and other legends: "I just feel very fortunate to be playing in the era that suits my style. Players like Phil Esposito, Bobby Hull, Bobby Orr, and Gordie Howe were great players and would have been great players in any era. I'm glad that the way the game's played now, I've been able to join them, sort of."

On his slender build: "I look like the guy who bags your groceries at the supermarket."

On his vision on the ice: "When I'm on the ice I can barely see the goalie. If you ask a 50-goal scorer what the goalie looks like, he'll say the goalie's just a blur. Ask a 5-goal scorer and he'll say the goalie looks like a huge glob of pads. I'm seeing the net, he's seeing the pads."

On Steve Kasper of the Bruins, a "shadow" who played Gretzky especially tough: "Nobody played better defense on me than Kasper. When I got married I half expected to see Kasper standing at the altar in a tux."

On his shot: "I don't think you have to put a hole in the boards. Some guys have missiles for shots, but if it takes three months to load up and fire, what good is it?"

On his priorities in life: "Hockey is just a game, my family comes first."

On fighting: "I know fighting brings some people into the building. But how many people does fighting keep out of the building?"

On playing hockey: "I cannot imagine doing anything else."

WAYNE TALKS TRASH

Don Cherry once described Wayne Gretzky as "the social con-
science of hockey," for his principled stands against fighting and
the way he conducts himself in life. True enough. But let's not
forget, Gretzky is a fierce competitor who hates to lose. He's
hardly a saint, as he'd be the first to tell you, and some of his state-
ments about opponents and others can be rather un-Gretzkylike.
Some examples of the immodest side of Mr. G:

On former Islanders star Mike Bossy: "I always respected
Bossy for his shot, but I wouldn't be too excited to share a cab
with him. Maybe if I knew him outside of hockey, I'd like
him, but I don't know: In his book, he picked himself on his
all time NHL team, which I think is a monument to self-
importance."

On a poor New Jersey Devils team: "They're putting a Mickey
Mouse operation on the ice. They better start getting some better personnel. It's ruining hockey."

After this remark caused a furor in New Jersey, Gretzky commented: "You'd have thought I'd criticized Miss Newark or something."

On hockey writer Stan Fischler: "He's got everybody in New
York thinking he's an expert on the game. The truth is, he's not
very knowledgeable. He once told me that I should not take anything he writes seriously, since most of the time he was just saying things to rile people up."

On one of his coaches in junior hockey, Paul Theriault: "Theriault immediately set out to change my style. He wanted me to
be in exactly the right place all the time, which is exactly the
wrong place for me. I go where the puck is going, not where it
was. To make me play in a certain spot in a certain time was like
taking one of my skates off. I hated the guy."

On the hockey "shadows" assigned to cover him during a
game: "Shadows usually aren't too bright. If I suddenly went into
the men's room, they'd probably follow me there."

On having a Wayne Gretzky doll manufactured in his likeness: "I hated that doll. Every arena I'd go to on the road, that doll would be hanging from somebody's noose. Or on fire. Or both."

After Hall of Famer Rocket Richard said that Gretzky wouldn't have scored as many goals if he had played in the "old days," Wayne responded: "I admire Rocket Richard, but he is still angry that Gordie [Howe] passed him. In every other sport almost everybody admits that performance is better now than it was twenty years ago. For some reason though, hockey has a hard time keeping up with the calendar."

GRETZKY THE COMPETITOR

Two brief anecdotes further illustrate Gretzky's hotly competitive nature. In his first year with the Los Angeles Kings, Gretzky broke his stick against a goalpost in disgust. Coach Robbie Ftorek, saying he wanted to teach Gretzky a lesson, benched him. Gretzky immediately confronted Ftorek: "Robbie, we're trying to win a Stanley Cup. If you want to teach, go back to New York." Gretzky has denied making this remark, but he's never denied teaching a lesson to goalie Jim Craig, the star of Team USA's "Miracle on Ice" triumph in the 1980 Winter Olympics. Craig joined the Atlanta Flames the season after the Olympics, and soon found himself in goal in a game against the Great One. "Hey Gretzky," Craig jabbed, "who the hell do you think you are anyway?" Gretzky scored two goals and two assists in thirty minutes. "I think Jim Craig learned that actions speak louder than words in the NHL," said Gretzky afterwards.

A HERO'S LIFE: THE EARLY YEARS

Wayne Gretzky was the Mozart of hockey. Not merely gifted or talented, but a hockey prodigy, a genius on the ice. He was shooting wrist shots at "Wally Coliseum," his father's homemade back-

yard ice rink, when other children were still learning to walk. It's
no wonder that some people—other players, the parents of other
players—resented him at first. "He got used to being famous at
a young age," wrote one of his many biographers. Nonetheless,
fame did not come without a price tag attached to it.

When he was a kid, making the other kids look bad just by
showing up on the same ice with them, Gretzky often got razzed.
"Puck hog" and "hot dogger" were two of the names they called
him. His coaches were accused of favoring him over the other,
less-gifted, players, though you'd have to be blind to ignore a talent such as Gretzky's and not want to see, as a coach, that talent
blossom and fully express itself. But anyone involved in youth
athletics knows how irrational parents, and sometimes their children, can become. At the age of fourteen, Gretzky was booed by
his hometown fans of Brantford, Canada. That same year he wore
white gloves when he played. "What's he need those gloves for?"
the fans heckled. "He ain't playing at night!" Gretzky's choice of
99 as his number—it was very unusual then for hockey players
to have high numbers—was another subject of razzing: "Hey
Gretzky," the fans would shout, "this ain't football . . . thirteen,
seventy-two, hike!"

One of Wayne's nicknames as a kid was "Pencil," because he
was as thin as one. Watching his son play against twenty-year-
olds while still only fourteen—the young Gretzky was always
playing against older kids—his father remarked that he looked
"like a calf in a herd of buffalo." Learning to survive—and
thrive—in the buffalo herd, Gretzky played a different brand of
hockey than the rest. At the age of sixteen, at his first Junior A
practice in Sault Ste. Marie, Gretzky asked coach Muzz
MacPherson how many points had won the league scoring title
the previous season. Muzz answered "170" and Gretz responded:
"No problem. I'll break that." Ted Williams, when asked about
his ambitions as a ballplayer, exhibited a similar sort of cockiness,
saying, "I want to be the greatest hitter that ever lived." But, like
Williams, Gretzky had the goods to back up what he said. The

sixteen-year-old wunderkind scored 182 points that season and
led the league.

THREE PRACTICAL JOKES THAT GRETZKY'S TEAMMATES
PLAYED ON HIM AFTER HE JOINED THE PROS

1) Eyebrows shaved. His eyebrows were painted on for four
weeks, until they grew back.

2) Shaving cream in his hair while sleeping on a jet. Gretzky
woke up, then got all the way to baggage claim before realizing
his head was a gooey white mop.

3) Shoes stolen on a flight. One time he walked barefoot
through an entire airport; no one would tell him where his shoes
were.

A HERO'S LIFE: THE OILER YEARS

Wayne Gretzky signed with the upstart World Hockey Association as an upstart seventeen-year-old. Clearly the kid was a great
talent, but some questioned his courage—whether he could
physically withstand the more arduous pro game. "Early in his
career he did a lot of talking," says goalie Richard Brodeur. "He
had a reputation as a crybaby." Gretzky scored a total of 29 goals
against Brodeur, making him one of the two biggest victims in
Wayne's prodigious goal-scoring career, but the old goalie is not
just talking trash. Gretzky's reputation as a "whiner" has dogged
him his entire career. Then again, at age seventeen, Gretzky was
only 161 pounds. When he got hit it probably did hurt.

The Edmonton Oilers of the WHA, owned by Peter Pocklington, purchased Gretzky's contract for $850,000. Goalie Eddie
Mio and winger Peter Driscoll were part of the historic package.
"They paid $849,999.99 for Gretz and one cent for me and Pe-
ter," joked Mio. Gretzky immediately began earning back this investment, burning up the WHA just as he had burned up the

juniors and peewees. But questions about his toughness, and his
abilities when matched up against the world's best players in the
NHL, remained. "Sure he can play junior varsity hockey," one
critic scoffed, "but what will happen when he gets to the NHL?"

In 1979, when the WHA merged with the NHL, Gretzky gave
a thunderous answer. "The NHL's muckamucks echoed the same
skepticism of Gretzky that he'd heard since his days in junior
hockey," recalls Stephen Hanks, a Gretzky biographer. "The kid's
too small, the kid's too scrawny. The kid won't withstand the tough
checking in the NHL. The kid will be lucky to score 20 goals." At
age eighteen, Gretzky scored 51 goals and tied for the league
scoring title in his first NHL season.

Still, some people weren't convinced: "Yes, he's a big goal
scorer," they said, "but he wouldn't score as many if he were playing for a winning team." In 1984, the year the Oilers won their
first Stanley Cup, Gretzky was a one-man scoring hurricane,
blowing away the opposition with 13 goals and 22 assists in nineteen playoff games. The Oilers went on to win four Cups in five
years, with Gretzky in the eye of the hurricane the whole way.

Those great Oiler teams changed the face of hockey. Though
they were as tough as anybody, they showed that there was more
to the game than simply bashing somebody à la the Philadelphia
Flyers. Still, in those early years before the championships, there
were plenty of doubters. In 1981 the lowly Oilers drew the
mighty Montreal Canadiens in the first round. The Canadiens
had little respect for the "weak-kneed wimps" from the West.
Montreal goalie Richard Sevigny said that Guy LaFleur was going to put the vaunted Gretzky "in his back pocket." Uh, sorry.
Didn't quite work that way. In the first game, Edmonton smashed
the Canadiens in the Forum, 6–3, and Gretzky got five assists, a
playoff record. After the Oilers' sixth goal Gretzky skated past Sevigny in net and—making sure the goalie saw him—patted his,
uh, back pockets.

After dispatching Montreal in three straight, Gretzky said the
Oilers were thrilled to beat "the best team in hockey"—a nice

compliment to the vanquished Canadiens, but not so nice for the New York Islanders, their next opponent. "For all his precocious genius on the ice, Wayne Gretzky is indisputably twenty years old in coping with the psychology of playoff diplomacy," wrote Dave Anderson in the *New York Times*. "By complimenting the Canadiens, he unthinkingly has insulted the Islanders." The Islanders were working on a dynasty of their own and they summarily ended Edmonton's—and Gretzky's—playoff run.

Some people thought Gretzky and Co. were wimps at first. When the Oilers proved them wrong, the critics turned around and called them "arrogant." After Edmonton won it all in 1984, *Inside Sports* predicted its reign as the best team in hockey would be short-lived. "It's only a one-year dynasty for Gretzky and Team Arrogance," the magazine sniffed. That proved wrong too, but the Oilers did take a cue from their best player and toned down their act in subsequent years. "Last year we were so cocky," admitted one Edmonton player. "The phrase we use this year is: 'Let's quietly annihilate the other team and get out of town.'"

And so they did, proving people wrong as they went. For many years the New York Islanders seemed to have Gretzky's number. "Gretzky was mostly manacled by his foes and betrayed by his weaknesses," observed Stan Fischler, who has not always been kind to the Great One. "The Islanders subdued Gretzky merely by persistent checking." The Islanders checked and frustrated Gretzky, and until 1984, stopped him from scoring when they faced one another in the playoffs. One joke making the rounds among Islander fans went like this:

Q: "What do Mickey Mouse and Wayne Gretzky have in common?"

A: "Neither has scored against the Islanders in the Stanley Cup."

But Gretzky broke the jinx by scoring in the fourth game of the Oilers' 1984 series against the Islanders, and Edmonton skated away with its first Stanley Cup, the first of many to come.

How Wayne Became "the Great One"

Gretzky has as many nicknames as he does scoring titles (well, almost). In junior hockey they called him "Ink," because he got so much of it from the press, and "Pencil," because he was skinny as one. They also called him "Pretzel," because, said his father, he was so skinny, his opponents thought they could break him in half. Fat chance. Wayne himself said they called him "Pretzel" because he skated "all hunched over" when he was a kid.

Gretzky got his most famous nickname—"the Great One"—at the age of 10, after he scored a zillion goals or so in a youth hockey season. "A writer hung that on me. I didn't really like the name then and it still embarrasses me now. My friends call me 'Gretz,'" recalls the Great—uh, Gretz. Whether he likes it or not, "the Great One" is the nickname that will stay with him forever, *because he is*. Though occasionally the name comes back to haunt him. After watching Gretzky during a bad streak with the Kings, the writer Allan Malamud commented, "The way he's playing, his nickname ought to be downgraded to 'the Good One.'"

The Trade

Ah yes, "the Trade." No true hockey fan and certainly no resident of Edmonton, Alberta, needs to have that reference explained to them. Nevertheless, there may be a few souls out there who have only recently discovered hockey and who may need to get up to speed. For this, we turn to the always urbane Trent Frayne, who puts it in a nutshell: "It is not a closely guarded secret that the most celebrated hockey player of the 1980s was Wayne Gretzky, the national treasure dealt off to Los Angeles by the meat-packer owner of the Edmonton Oilers, Peter Pocklington, who, unimpeded by sentiment or passion, may have mistook him for a side of pork."

The Trade occurred on August 9, 1988. It was like Babe Ruth

being sold to the Yankees. The Edmonton Oilers, winner of the four of the past five Stanley Cups, had sent the greatest player in hockey history to Surf City, USA. One struggles to find the appropriate word to describe the reaction of hockey fans. Shock? When the Japanese invaded Pearl Harbor in 1941, that was a shock. No, this was beyond shock. This was . . . *huge.*

People in Canada were bummed (to use a Surf City term) because for them, Gretzky wasn't just a hockey player, he was a national hero. In the 1981–82 season, perhaps his greatest season, in which he became the first player to score 50 goals in fewer than fifty games, no less than thirteen songs were written about him by admiring, though possibly tone-deaf, Canadians. Sending Gretzky to LA was unthinkable. It was as if Canada had decided to trade in the maple leaf for palm trees and sand. Here's columnist Jim Taylor, writing an article entitled "A Nation in Mourning" for *Sports Illustrated*: "Forget the controversy over whether No. 99 jumped or was pushed; the best hockey player in the world was ours, and the Americans flew up from Hollywood in their private jet and bought him. It wasn't the Canadian heart that was torn, it was the Canadian psyche that was ripped. In the minds of Edmontonians and Canadian hockey fans everywhere, Gretzky had been theirs to keep." Taylor added, "If this be free trade, stuff it."

In the long run, the Trade may have been the best thing that ever happened to hockey in the United States. Hockey had long been big in the Eastern U.S. and parts of the Midwest, but suddenly, the game's greatest celebrity was in Hollywood, the land of celebrities. With Gretzky starring for the Los Angeles Kings, hockey became more of a national game than it had ever been before. His presence helped pave the way for expansion franchises in Anaheim, San Jose, and other parts of the U.S. As San Francisco sportswriter Lowell Cohn notes, "Gretzky isn't the greatest hockey player of the last decade and a half. He *is* hockey of the last decade and a half. The San Jose Arena [home of the Sharks] is just another House That Wayne Built."

"People who say he wasn't—or isn't—the greatest player in hockey, are nuts."—*Barry Melrose*. Photo courtesy of the Los Angeles Kings

But this was little consolation for Canadians, upset over the buying and selling of their No. 1 citizen. Paul Coffey, the former Oiler great playing for Pittsburgh, charged that his former teammate had been treated "like a piece of meat." Some immediately blamed Janet Jones, Gretzky's new wife, a Hollywood actress who, they said, turned young Wayne's head and secretly engineered the trade so she could pursue her career. "Jezebel Janet," "witch," and "Dragon Lady" were some of the printable comments they made about her. As events would show, the charges were poppycock. Jones herself put it this way at the time: "Owners just don't make $15 million trades for wives," she said. "Peter Pocklington is the reason Wayne Gretzky is no longer an Edmonton Oiler. I know the real story. I know the whole story."

The whole story can, of course, be summed up in one word: money. Bruce McNall, the owner of the Kings, had lots of it; Peter Pocklington, the owner of the Oilers, wanted some of it; and No. 99 was the way he was going to get it. Though this was not the way the story was first presented to a disbelieving public. Ac-

cording to Pocklington, McNall approached him about Gretzky.
Then when Pocklington asked Gretzky what he wanted to do,
Gretz said "Hollywood here I come," or words to that effect. This
was utter baloney. In fact, Pocklington had been shopping his top
commodity around the league for a couple of months. Later, when
Gretzky found out about this, he was stunned: "I'd been loyal as
hell to the Oilers, busted my butt, been part of one of the greatest dynasties in hockey history, and here I was getting thrown
around from team to team like a piece of meat," he wrote in his
autobiography.

Nor did Gretzky's teammates believe the Pocklington version
of events. "No way did Wayne want to leave Edmonton," said
Coffey in Pittsburgh. Wayne Mio agreed that his good friend
wanted to stay and defended Janet Jones, the unfairly persecuted
wife: "There's no bloody way he wanted to leave. I don't care if
he married the Queen of England," said Mio. "It was only after
the papers were drawn up that Wayne decided he'd had enough
of Peter Pocklington. And nobody should blame Janet for this
move. She does not deserve to be persecuted, not for one
minute."

Edmonton fans hung Pocklington in effigy outside Northlands
Coliseum and threatened a boycott against his meat and dairy
businesses. But nothing they could do would bring Wayne back.
At his farewell press conference Gretzky broke down and cried,
and Pocklington, in his own press conference, implied that
Wayne was acting. Gretzky heard about this and told a magazine
interviewer: "And I hear that he says I faked the tears. I was the
most pissed off I've ever been at a person in my whole life. Over
the past ten years, I had played in every exhibition game and
never missed a promotional appearance. I had done everything
he'd ever asked me to do, and we'd won four Stanley Cups. For
him to throw all that away with one silly remark didn't make
sense."

To many Canadians, the Trade will never make sense. But in
characteristic Gretzky fashion, he said that he remains a Cana-

dian boy at heart . "I'm still proud to be a Canadian," he has said. "I didn't desert my country. I moved because I was traded and that's where my job is. But I'm Canadian to the core. I hope that all Canadians understand that."

ROTTEN THINGS THAT WAYNE HAS SAID ABOUT PETER, AND PETER ABOUT WAYNE

"Peter Pocklington worries about nothing but the bottom line."
—Wayne Gretzky

"A great actor."
—Peter Pocklington, on No. 99 after his farewell press conference from Edmonton

"An ego the size of Manhattan."
—Peter Pocklington, on Gretzky

"I don't think he knew squat about hockey."
—Wayne Gretzky, on Pocklington

A HERO'S LIFE: THE LOS ANGELES YEARS

Glen Sather, Gretzky's coach in Edmonton, said once, "A fire hydrant could get 40 goals playing with Wayne Gretzky." After moving over to the Los Angeles Kings, Gretzky got more of a chance to play with fire hydrants than ever before. Still, he *was* Gretzky. In his first year with the team he won another Hart Trophy as the league MVP, despite scoring 168 points to Mario Lemieux's 199. Mario groused about this—"Nothing in this league makes sense," he grumbled. "In the past they gave it to the best player or top scorer. I don't know why it should change"—but the award recognized the fact that Gretzky helped turn the one-time "Queens" into winners. With Gretzky leading the way, the Kings jumped from 18th place in the league to fourth and—ah, revenge is sweet—upset Edmonton in the first round of the 1989 playoffs.

The Kings came to be known as "the Bruce and Wayne Show," referring to Bruce McNall, the big-bucks owner who brought Wayne to LA. But it was mostly always Wayne's World. After missing the first part of the season due to a herniated disc, "His Greatness" roared back to lead the Kings to their first Stanley Cup finals in 1993. "Gretzky toyed with us tonight," Montreal coach Jacques Demers said after the Kings whipped the Canadiens in one game. But Gretzky did not toy with the Canadiens quite enough during that series, and Montreal won in five.

The following season the Kings played like serfs, plunging precipitously into the lower strata of NHL society. After nearly winning it all in 1993, they didn't even make the playoffs in 1994. "They have a whole lot of talent, but they didn't seem to have any direction," said one rival player. Kings coach Barry Melrose was more evocative, describing LA's season as "Nightmare on Manchester." Those weren't Kings players in those silver-and-black uniforms, they were fright-show impostors. "Freddy Krueger showed up," said Melrose. "Jason showed up. Dracula, Frankenstein. The bride of Frankenstein." Added Melrose, who may be watching too many horror movies, "You feel like Dracula, like a stake's been driven through your heart. It's awful, a terrible time in your life."

It was equally terrible for Kings players. "We lay down like dogs and there's no excuse for it," said Pat Conacher after the team found out it had missed the playoffs. "You can't print the words I'm thinking now. My God, have some pride. Whether we win, lose or draw, play your guts out and don't lay down and be beaten like a dog. Go out like a man, not like a whipped dog." Whipped dogs, Dracula, Bride of Frankenstein, stakes in the heart—man, those Kings really did have a bad year.

Nevertheless, as always has been and always will be the case, the Great One stood above the rest. While breaking Gordie Howe's all-time goal scoring record, Gretzky put together one of his best-ever seasons despite the presence of so many fire hydrants around him. "The greatest player in the game is giving everything he's got, the rest of us are giving nothing, and it's absolutely disgusting," Conacher continued. "To have a player like that who gives and gives and gives, and then to get no help . . . We should be truly ashamed of ourselves." You said it, Pat.

MUTUAL ADMIRATION SOCIETY

"Gordie Howe was cool. Not only was he this great player who scored more than anybody else, he looked cool, with his hair always perfectly slicked back and those eagle eyes staring holes in people."

—Wayne Gretzky, on Gordie Howe

"When someone has done what this kid has done, he doesn't have to say anything."

—Gordie Howe, on Wayne Gretzky

FAN MAIL

Wayne Gretzky gets a ton of fan mail. But this was one of the best pieces he ever received. After he scored the 1,851st point of his career, Wayne got this telegram from the late comedian John Candy:

"CONGRATULATIONS ON THIS TREMEN-DOUS MILESTONE IN YOUR CAREER. BUT DON'T THINK YOU'RE IN A LEAGUE BY YOUR-

SELF. I PLAYED 18 HOLES ONCE AND SHOT
1,851. YOUR FAITHFUL FAN, JOHN CANDY."

FINAL THOUGHTS ON WAYNE

*"People who say that he wasn't—or isn't—the greatest player
in hockey, are nuts."*

—Barry Melrose

4

THE FIGHTING-EST GAME AROUND

The sportswriter John Kieran once wrote, "For fighting fast and free, grab your hat and come with me./ And for ground and lofty smacking and enthusiastic whacking,/ Give me hockey—I'll take hockey—any time!" Indeed. Hockey is the fastest and fighting-est sport in the world. Although the NHL has made an effort in recent years to clean up its act and cut down on the fisticuffs, fighting remains as much a part of hockey as sticks and pucks.

WHY HOCKEY PLAYERS FIGHT

"Either you give it right back or the next thing you know, everybody and his brother will be trying you on for size."
> —Doug Harvey, All-Star defenseman

"Hockey is our bread and butter. You're going to think twice before you let another fellow take it away from you."
> —More from Doug Harvey, on why he drops the gloves

"I've been slashed, speared, elbowed, butt-ended and board-checked as much as anybody who ever played. I had a broken shoulder, broken instep, broken hand, and a couple of hundred stitches in my face. I just want to keep the ledger balanced."
—Hall of Famer Ted Lindsay, on his eye-for-an-eye fighting philosophy

"If I play badly I'll pick a fight in the third period just to get into a fight. I'll break a guy's leg to win, I don't care. Afterward I'll say, 'All right I played badly, but I won the fight, so who gives a damn.'"
—Derek Sanderson, onetime Boston bad boy

"It's not who wins the fight that's important, it's being willing to fight. If you get challenged and renege, everyone will take a shot at you."
—Ex-hockey enforcer Barclay Plager, who seldom reneged

"Hockey is a physical sport and fighting is a natural outlet for all the on-ice aggression. Other than the score, fighting can sometimes be the only way to settle matters."
—Eric Lindros, of the Philadelphia Flyers

FIGHTING (PRO)

"I think the odd scrap—without sticks—is part of the game."
—Bobby Orr, Hall of Famer

"Fights are inevitable with spirited men."
—Billy Reay, former Blackhawk coach

"I'm not going to condemn my players for fighting. That's what they're supposed to do when challenged, or they'd be run out of the league."
>—More thoughts on fighting from Billy Reay

"What a great game! What a great game! Three fights and you guys won them all. Way to go, guys! No running for you today!"
>—Coach Bill LaForge, to his players after a fight-filled game

"Hockey is hitting people. What's all the fuss about?"
>—Brown University hockey coach Mary Leslie Ullman, when her team was accused of rough play in an Ivy League game

FIGHTING (CON)

"Hockey is the only team sport in the world that actually encourages fighting. The game itself is so fast, so exciting, so much fun to watch, why do we have to turn the ice red so often? Why do the best shots in a game have to be on somebody's nose instead of on somebody's net?"
>—Wayne Gretzky, long an opponent of fighting in hockey

"It does not take bravery to hit another man over the head with a stick. If you want to fight, go to France."
>—1917 dictum of Toronto coach Charlie Querrie

"The finest game in the world to watch, hockey, is being made a byword and a disgrace by the manner in which matches are con-

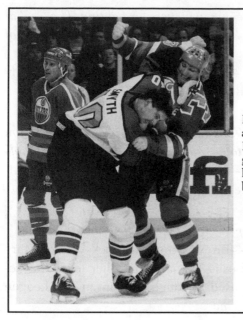

Fellas, fellas, can we talk about this, please? Messrs. McSorley and Smyth engage in a meaningful dialogue with their fists. Photo by Bruce Bennett

ducted and foul play tolerated. Unless a radical change occurs at once in the conduct of hockey matches, the noble winter sport of Canada must sink in the public estimation to the level of pugilism."
                                        —*Ottawa Evening Journal,* 1904

"*Hockey is the greatest game in the world without fighting and violence. The attitudes fostered in the NHL filter down to the juniors and kids. If we're trying to teach our children the right values in life, then it's something we should be concerned about."*
                                        —Bruce Hood, former NHL referee

"*So many fights are needless. Many times players don't even want to fight but do because they have to keep up the image of being a rough, tough hockey player."*
                                        —More from Bruce Hood on why he thinks fighting should be banned

"I'll fight anybody, but to me it's a waste of time and energy. Swinging the arms takes a lot out of a guy. By the time a guy's through fighting he doesn't have any power left to score."

—Hall of Fame winger Frank Mahovlich, when he was playing

"I had never liked the fights. The famous tactic—the primary one apparently—of reaching around behind the opponent, detaching his suspenders and pulling his jersey up over his shoulders and head so that he could not see the punches coming . . . all of this offered very little aesthetic pleasure. It was difficult (for me at least) to feel much more than disgust. The dismay was increased by the apparent liking of many of my neighbors for what they were seeing—shouting for more mayhem, the mood everywhere in the arena so ugly."

—George Plimpton, writer

"It's not the chance fight that one is concerned about. It's the staged roller derby-wrestling–Show Biz scrap that league officials think is box office and is just dandy. More: it's the fight as intimidation, a strategy to even things up when the other side is too talented, too fast, too good."

—Jack Ludwig, novelist

"In that fighting skews hockey's image the way a pornographic bookstore sets the mood for a neighborhood, why does the NHL permit it?"

—Joe LaPointe, sportswriter

Great Moments in Ring—uh, Rink History

The history of hockey is filled with the stories of great fights. Players have died as a result of fights on the ice. One critic denounced a 1907 game between Montreal and Ottawa as "an exhibition of butchery." A Quebec judge at the time noted that the violent be-

havior that routinely occurred in hockey rinks would not have
been permitted on Canada's streets, and that hockey players
seemed to think they were above the law. In fact, hockey players
were simply obeying another law: the law of survival in a very
tough game. Here are some accounts of bloody hockey battles:

*"Heads were bashed, benches smashed, and lady spectators
fled in confusion."*
> —Hockey historian J.W. Fitsell, describ-
> ing the first-ever indoor hockey game
> ever played, in 1875 in Montreal

*"I've never seen more damage done by one man to another in
my life. After they revived him Wilson needed enough stitches in
him to weave an Indian blanket."*
> —Hall of Famer Newsy Lalonde, on a fight
> between Dick Irvin and Cully Wilson

*"The two started shoving and the action ended when Meeker
picked Leswick up in a crotch hold, threw him to the ice with a
body slam and with Meeker on top of him, Leswick's head hit the
ice."*
> —An account of a fight between New
> York's Tony Leswick and Toronto's Howie
> Meeker

*"The usually mild-mannered Toronto winger [Harry Watson]
went berserk. He shed his gloves and peppered Boston defenseman Murray Henderson with a series of hard, short jabs to the
face. Watson landed at least eight blows and Henderson was
forced to retire to the Boston dressing room with a flattened nose."*
> —Toronto sportswriter Jim Vipond

"He came out looking like the loser of a saber duel at Stuttgart."
> —Former hockey great Frank Boucher, watching Hall of Famer Jack Adams get manhandled in a fight

"Joe DiMaggio, Willie Mays, and Stan Musial never swung harder than the two players doing their macabre dance around the rink. Soon, blood burst forth from their respective faces. They looked like a pair of gored bulls."
> —Stan Fischler, witnessing a hockey fight

"The Montreal rear guard [Kenny Reardon] applied a full nelson on Ezinicki twice within a matter of seconds. Butch Bouchard boarded Joe Klukay and then climbed on the Toronto player's back, jockey style. Murph Chamberlain joined the fray, and when a spectator grabbed a stick, the terrible-tempered Mr. Chamberlain slashed wildly across the boards, narrowly missing a woman's head."
> —Jim Vipond, Toronto sportswriter, on a 1940s-era fight between the Canadiens and Maple Leafs

"After breaking their sticks on each other, they continued to attack with the splintered shafts in a bloody brawl that left each with forty stitches. 'Evans hacked me,' remembers Zeidel, 'but I hung in there and battled him. He couldn't put me away. I was swinging and missing. He was swinging and hitting. He carved me up.'"
> —From *Hockey*, a recounting of a minor league brawl between Jack Evans and Larry "the Rock" Zeidel

"Richard lashed a jolting right and it found a target on Juzda's left eye. Juzda dropped heavily and lay on the ice for almost a full minute."

> —Sportswriter Gord Walker's account
> of a Rocket Richard TKO

"The Moe-Durnan and Laycoe-Lamoureux bouts were ortho- dox boxing exhibitions. Richard broke his stick over Juzda's head and Juzda swarmed in and wrestled him to the ice. Bouchard ripped Hextall's stick away from him and flattened him with a punch. Moe broke a stick over Bouchard's head and Bouchard didn't seem to notice that he had been hit. When it was over Rear- don had ten stitches in his face, the bald-headed spectator had three stitches, and Buddy O'Connor had a fractured cheekbone, allegedly a result of being hit by Juzda's stick."

> —Columnist Jim Coleman, on a Ranger-
> Canadien donnybrook

"So I jumped on him and hit him a few more times and nobody broke us up. Finally I got up off him and saw him twitching there, out cold. The twitching frightened me. I knew every time I had hit him his head hit the ice and I figured he was in pretty bad shape. But then my natural instincts took over and I said to myself, 'So what?'"

> —Derek Sanderson, recalling a fight he
> was in in junior hockey

"I was exhausted, but my fury still wasn't spent. As the referee grabbed me by the neck and pulled me away, I fell backwards to a point where my left skate blade lifted directly over McKey's head. For that split second it crossed my mind that I could bring my sharp blade down, guillotine-style, over his head."

> —Denis Potvin, describing a fight in ju-
> nior hockey with Fran McKey (who kept
> his head, but was injured)

"The only time I ever saw more blood was the day I was taken on a tour of the cattle-killing floor of an abattoir."

> —Jim Coleman, after a vicious fight in which a player split open another player's head with a hockey stick

"The puck was dropped to open the game, and it went into the corner and Rosey went after it, only to be cross-checked in the back of the neck by Brophy, as if to say 'Hey, Kid, my name is Brophy.' Brophy was more formally introduced to Paiement when Rosey turned around and hit him eight times before Brophy knew a fight was on. The resulting brawl was one of the classics of all time. Forty minutes later, and after reading off penalties for about another six minutes, the P.A. announcer finished with . . . 'And the time: six seconds.'"

> —Broadcaster Gene Hart, recounting a mid-sixties brawl between Rosaire Paiement ("Rosey") and John Brophy in an exhibition game

HARD CHECKS

Hard checking is not fighting; a hard check is considered well within the rules by everyone. (Okay, sometimes players bend the rules a little when they mash somebody.) Still, a hard check is a violent act. "The teams went at one another fiercely," wrote one Ottawa sportswriter, describing a turn-of-the-century hockey game. "There was no letup from the very start to the last minute, and no mercy was shown in the checking with body and stick." There never is, in hockey. Men collide, they go down, get smashed into the boards, fly into the air, and frequently they get hurt. Here are some graphic descriptions of some really hard checks and physical blows:

"I got one penalty for tripping and another for boarding. In the boarding call I really clotheslined the guy with my arm. His body went one way and his head just stayed put."

—Brad Park, former New York Ranger defenseman

"Defenseman Guy LaPointe really creamed me. His check was a beating. Up in the air like a rocket, then down on my head like a bomb."

—Brad Park, showing that he could admire a good, hard check even when he was the victim

"Walker's goal was followed by one of the crudest and most brutal assaults seen on the ice here. Boucher, the bad man of the NHL, jumped into Walker and smashed the veteran into the boards. Walker staggered for a second but collapsed unconscious."

—*Victoria Daily Times*, on a hard Billy Boucher check on Jack Walker

"I remember one night with the Leafs we were playing the Canadiens, and Sylvio Mantha was the key to their defense. Dick Irvin was coach for us then, and he called me over to the bench. 'Get that Mantha,' he told me. First chance I got I caught him with a cross-check and broke his jaw."

—King Clancy, recalling a game from the 1930s

"Bobby Hull set the style by smashing into the Leafs' Bobby Baun three times. They crashed with the impact of railway engines."

—Red Burnett, sportswriter, at a Leafs-Blackhawks game

"A split second later Jack was really creamed by Fred Barrett, the tough rookie defenseman. Jack toppled over, hitting his head on the ice with a tremendous wallop. Instinctively we all knew Jack was in trouble, big trouble. Jack had swallowed his tongue

*and was within minutes of choking to death. [The trainer] had a
pair of tongs, forced Jack's mouth, and finally got his tongue out
of his mouth."*

> —Brad Park, witnessing a brutal check
> put on Ranger teammate Jack Egers in
> the early seventies

A "Check" Defined

Those fans who are new to the game of hockey may be confused
about what a "check" actually is, and how it differs, say, from getting mugged. Scott Ostler, the very entertaining San Francisco
sportswriter, explains it all for you:

"'Check,' he writes, "is a French-Canadian word that means
'to gouge in the eye with the sharpened end of the hockey stick.'
A check is not properly executed, in the eyes of a Canadian, unless something breaks, preferably something belonging to the
checkee. When Canadian hockey fans talk about crunch time,"
Ostler continues, "they mean it literally."

By way of illustration, Ostler points to a check performed during a recent Stanley Cup playoff game between Toronto and San
Jose. Writes Ostler: "A nice crisp check is like the one that Toronto's
Rob Pearson applied to Sandis Ozolinsh, when Pearson slammed
Ozolinsh (cleanly) to the boards, then executed the textbook fol-
low-through by assisting Ozolinsh to the ice with two hearty blows
to the back of the head." Now *that*, hockey fans, is a check.

What the Hockey Establishment Privately Thinks about Fighting

*"The big wheels of the NHL figure they have to have blood to
fill the arenas. During my years in the league that was all they
were interested in."*

> —Jack Mehlenbacher, retired NHL
> referee

"The fans are being used. Some of them enjoy the violence, but that doesn't mean they would not prefer displays of the athletic skill for which it is substituted. What the owners are saying is: 'It doesn't matter whether we give the suckers a good hockey game as long as we give them a fight.'"
　　　　　　　　　　　　　　　　　　　　—John MacFarlane, author

"Yes, we've got to stamp out this sort of thing [fighting] or people are going to keep on buying tickets."
　　　　　　　　　　　　　　　　　　　　—Conn Smythe, Toronto owner

HOW AMERICANS AND CANADIANS VIEW FIGHTING: ONE MAN'S OPINION

Do Canadians and Americans view fighting in hockey differently? Brad Park, formerly of the New York Rangers, thinks so. Said Park: "Canadians and Americans differ about hockey fighting. The Canadian is inclined to deplore it because he knows how the game should

Tie Domi shows why he is one of the baddest—and scariest—dudes in hockey. Ouch! Photo by Scott Levy/Bruce Bennett Studios

be played. Fighting is *not* hockey . . . American fans are something else. Many of them cry for blood the minute the puck is dropped, and the night isn't complete without one full-scale brawl."

A Simple Rebuttal to Those Who Think Hockey Fights Are Fixed

"If hockey fights were fixed, I'd be in more of them."
> —Rod Gilbert, when he was with the Rangers

A Hockey Spitfight

You know about hockey fistfights, of course. Well, one time Philadelphia defenseman Rick Foley and New York Ranger coach Emile Francis engaged in a hockey spitfight. Madder than a hornet at the Rangers, Foley skated over to their bench and spit right at Francis. Then he spat at him again. And again. But Francis was not known as "the Cat" for nothing; he jumped out of the way of Foley's loogie-bombs and stayed dry.

Said Francis afterwards: "Foley spits like he plays hockey. He never hit me once."

How Tough Are Hockey Players?

Pretty darn tough, we'll say. And a heck of a lot tougher than athletes in some other professional sports. "Baseball players?" sniffed Reggie "Cement Head" Fleming. "Why, they don't play if they've got a hangnail." Hockey players will play even if their broken leg has a hangnail. "Their tolerance to pain is remarkable," commented an awestruck orthopedic surgeon, Dr. James Nicholas. "Hockey athletes are the most uncomplaining athletes I've met." One writer was far less complimentary, describing hockey players as "a strange species of marvelously durable brutes, men who are uniquely and superhumanly (or perhaps subhumanly) insensitive to pain."

Hockey players bang around the boards, fight, throw hard body checks, collide with people going full speed, get knocked down, get back up, suffer broken noses, bleed and, like the Eveready rabbit, frequently just keep going and going. Some vivid illustrations of hockey men's tolerance to pain:

"Westwick skated off the ice and walked to the dressing room with the bone protruding through the skin."
> —1903 newspaper account of a vicious slash on Ottawa's Harry Westwick (Rather than go to the hospital, Westwick told doctors to put his leg in a splint and he watched the rest of the game from the stands.)

"Silas Griffi's knee is swollen to twice the normal size, and he and Billie McGumsie were hardly able to stand on their skates toward the end. Every man was badly cut around the face, except Brown and Giroux. Phillips had no fewer than seven cuts on his face."
> —Montreal newspaper, describing a rough game in the early 1900s

"I broke my ankle and, see, there was nothing in the papers, because the club wanted to keep it quiet. I broke it and right afterwards a couple of other guys were hurt and Mr. Adams asked me to play. I wore a plaster cast and played."
> —Detroit defenseman Red Kelly, recalling how he played on a broken ankle for Jack Adams's Red Wings

"We're playing Toronto and in the first period Doug tangles with Gus Bodnar. That sonuvabitch Bodnar rammed his stick down Doug's throat. His mouth looked awful. Four teeth knocked out, bleeding like a stuck hog. When the next period began Doug in-

sisted on playing. He did play, in the second period and the last one. After each period he came back vomiting blood."

> —Blackhawk trainer Eddie Froelich, on how Doug Bentley of Chicago endured a fight with Gus Bodnar

"I grabbed it and squeezed it and put it back in place. It gave a little crunch and popped right in."

> —Ranger defenseman Jay Wells, popping his broken nose into place after a vicious high stick by Pavel Bure in the 1994 Stanley Cup finals

WHY HOCKEY PLAYERS ENDURE SO MUCH PAIN

"I expect to get clouted every so often because hitting is part of the game, and you either learn to live with it or find another job."
> —Brad Park, former Ranger defenseman

"When the Stanley Cup is at stake, I can stand any amount of pain."

> —Cyclone Taylor, early 1900s hockey star, who played in the Cup finals despite a three-inch gash in his foot

SMILING THROUGH THE PAIN

Since pain and blood and broken bones and head butts and open wounds and concussions and contusions and compound fractures are such a part of hockey—okay, maybe we're getting a little carried away here—the game contains a great deal of gallows humor. It's a way for players to cope. They laugh, they make jokes—while the trainer gives them that painkilling injection and the coach shoves them back onto the ice again. One time Rick MacLeish, a center for the Philadelphia Flyers, fell onto the ice and, in a horrific accident, the blade of a skate ripped his neck open. Doctors put it back together with eighty-eight stitches and "the Hawk," as he was known, returned to play again, only to be ribbed by his fellow players with this joke:

Question: "What's the difference between Hawk MacLeish and Frankenstein's monster?"

Answer: "Two stitches."

HOCKEY THEATRICS

It's important to remember that just because a hockey player is hit or goes down, it doesn't mean he is hurt. It *is* a show, after all. Not only do hockey players want to entertain you, the paying audience, but they most certainly want to catch the eye of the officials, in the hopes that these officials will slap a penalty on the

"I'd rather fight than score. Scoring is over in a second, but a good fight can last a while and you've got time to enjoy it."—*Dave Schultz.* Photo by Mel Di-Giacomo/Bruce Bennett Studios

player who so rudely knocked them down and thereby give their team a man advantage.

Toronto sportswriter Jim Coleman writes wonderfully about the play-acting of one Ken Mosdell, who received a hard check from a Leafs player and flopped onto the ice. "Mosdell's actions apparently were inspired by the impression that referee Gorgeous George Hayes is a devotee of the drama," said Coleman. "Mosdell died oftener than Camille, and at any second we expected him to dab his dry lips daintily with a cambric kerchief. All in all it was the best acting that Toronto has seen since John Gielgud trod the boards at the Royal Alex."

When it comes to hockey fights, one also delves into the shadowy realm of perception. One man's "smash to the face" is another man's "barely touched him." A perfect example of this phenomenon occurred when Toronto's Red Horner got knocked to the ice by a Chicago Blackhawk player named Doc Romnes.

Here is how one poetically minded Toronto sportswriter saw it: "We Torontians screamed for Romnes' punishment. Romnes got a minor. We knew then it was a mad world and we were its victims."

And here is how a Chicago sportswriter saw the same incident: "Romnes waved his stick at Horner and the big Canadian fainted."

5

HOCKEY GOONS, OR TOUGH GUYS WE LOVE TO HATE

In talking about a tough guy for the Toronto Maple Leafs, Conn Smythe said: "He hit, to hurt." There is no finer or more succinct description of a hockey tough guy. That doesn't mean they play outside the rules (although some of them do), or that they want to injure or maim the people they're up against (although yes, some of them want to do that too). What it means is that when one of these guys hit you, he wants you to *feel* it. Here are some portraits of hockey tough guys who hit to hurt:

THE BULLY BOYS OF PHILLY

The Philadelphia Flyers—the entire *team*—personified toughness in the middle 1970s. They won back-to-back Stanley Cups by playing tough, hard—and, some would say, violent—hockey. They knocked off the Big, Bad Bruins as the biggest and baddest club in hockey and the games between those teams were epic struggles on the order of *Frankenstein Meets the Wolf Man* or Arnold versus the *evil* Terminator in *Terminator 2*. "I couldn't sleep before I played the Bruins," said Dave Schultz, the chief enforcer on the Flyers. "Our team has tough guys and their team has tough guys, but four of their tough guys are nuts." People said the same thing about the Flyers.

"They look like reincarnations of Dracula," an awestruck, and perhaps even frightened, Montreal fan said, describing Schultz, Bob Kelly, and other members of the Broad Street Bullies. They were called the Bullies because they *were* bullies. Except in Philadelphia, where the championship-starved fans loved them, fans across the NHL hated them. "The Flyers went at the Islanders like seagulls diving for sardines," Larry Merchant wrote after watching one Philadelphia game. Sometimes it wasn't even that pretty. It resembled gladiator contests or—more aptly, perhaps—professional wrestling when the villainous Flyers came to town. "The Flyers don't want to fight you one on one," said Jerry "King Kong" Korab, who mixed it up on occasion with the Bullies. "They want to fight you nineteen to one." "Something should be done about this," said Detroit Red Wings coach Johnny Wilson. "They're letting brutality get into the game. They have lawsuits pending against them all over the league. All that holding and spearing doesn't make sense. You don't win hockey games playing like animals." Added Ranger defenseman Brad Park: "If I had to win that way, I don't want to win."

Philly's hard-nosed style was controversial, but it was also successful. NHL teams copied the Flyers' hard-nosed brand of hockey because a) the Flyers were winning, and b) they had no choice. It was either get some goons of your own, or get beat up. Still, it's not fair to say that the Flyers excelled in thuggery alone. They had some great talent (notably, the wondrous Bobby Clarke) and a coach who knew how to get the best out of his men. "I don't have the best players," Fred Shero liked to say. "I have the best team." Especially when Kate Smith, their inspirational chanteuse, came to sing.

"Coach Fred Shero's system was to create as much havoc as possible," said NHL referee Bruce Hood. Bobby Taylor, a backup goalie on the Bullies, agreed: "Freddie gave the impression of being detached from all the fighting and brawling that went on and the image the team had," said Taylor. "He looked like an innocent bystander, but he really did encourage it. His whole thing was Us against Them." Here, then, are profiles of a few of them—or, if you were a fan of the Bullies, Us.

The Hammer

"I'd rather fight than score," Dave Schultz said once. "Scoring is over in a second, but a good fight can last a while and you've got time to enjoy it." The Hammer had lots of fights to savor in his career. Standing 6-1 and weighing in at 190 pounds, Schultz was the fighting-est, brawling-est player on the fighting-est, brawling-est team in the history of the game. Schultz was as arrogant as they come. "I'll fight anybody or do anything," he said. "But nobody fools with my team." And nobody did. And if they did, Dave made an appointment with him. Crash!

"I'll tell you something about Dave Schultz," said Denis Potvin. "My old lady can punch a lot harder than him." Strangely, Potvin said this after getting into a fight with Schultz, a fight that Potvin lost. Maybe Schultz should have fought Potvin's old lady.

Ain't Nothin' but a Hound Dog

Bob "Hound" Kelly was Schultz's teammate on the Broad Street Bullies and "the most dangerous 11-goal scorer in hockey," according to a fellow Flyer. He was dangerous for the same reason Schultz was: he was a brawler. Kelly "dropped his gloves in a season more often than he put the puck in the net," D'Arcy Jenish has noted. But, as the Hound noted wisely, "they don't pay me to score goals." Flyers broadcaster Gene Hart compared him to the ball in a pinball machine—always bouncing off people. Boston Bruin enforcer John Wesnick crossed sticks with the Hound several times over the years, but actually came to like it. "The game can be dead boring," said Wesnick, "but when Hound steps on the ice, well, for sure, it's not dull anymore." You've got that right. "If a guy has the guts to try and maim me," said Kelly, "I'll try to maim him back."

For all his vaunted pugilistic abilities, Hound Kelly was not, by all reports, the brightest of men. Okay, he was dense as a potato. In the locker room din following a game, Kelly saw a man seated in his changing stall. "Hey old man, get out of my locker," Hound barked. "Pardon me?" said the old man. "Get outta my locker," Hound repeated. The old man—the Governor of Pennsylvania, Milton Shapp—did indeed move. Then there was that joke about Kelly that made the rounds:

Question: "What do a school and the Hockey Hall of Fame have in common?"

Answer: "Bob Kelly doesn't have a chance to get into either one."

Perhaps not, but a lot of very smart guys knew better than to mess with the Hound in a fight.

The Moose

Andre "Moose" Dupont was yet another tough guy on the Bullies—there were a lot of them, weren't there?—who often had trouble with English. He called teammate Bobby Taylor "Chef" and everybody thought that was because Taylor was a good cook. No, Moose meant to say "Chief," a reference to Taylor's Native American heritage. He called Toronto's Borje Salming "Swiss Cheese." When told that Borje was Swedish, not Swiss, the Moose said, "Same thing. Hey, Swiss Cheese! Swiss Cheese!"

But they didn't call Andre "the Moose" for nothing. He was big and ornery. A player who had just been acquired by the Flyers from Vancouver was skating around during warm-ups, when Dupont hit him with a body check, knocking him to the ice. "I just wanted to show you that you're not with those pansies in Vancouver anymore," Moose explained to his new teammate. After returning from a winning road trip against the Canucks, Moose expressed the sentiment of his Flyer teammates—indeed the whole Broad Street Bully philosophy: "Great trip for us. We don't go to jail. We beat up their chicken forwards. We score ten goals. We win. And," he added, throwing back a cool one, "now de Moose drinks beer."

The Rink Rat

Bobby Clarke was not a tough guy the way Dave Schultz or Bob Kelly was tough. But he was *mean*—and like Fred Shero, we mean that as a compliment. "Bobby Clarke is the ultimate as a competitor," said Shero. "Anybody who expects to be great has to be mean. I mean truly great like Gordie Howe, Rocket Richard, Milt Schmidt. They were mean." Sportswriter Mark Mulvoy described Clarke as "that tenacious gap-toothed diabetic rink rat, with the guts of ten dozen burglars."

Clarke was a great player, wonderfully talented, but he relished the Flyers' physical style as much as Schultz or anyone. "You don't have to be a genius to figure out what we do," said Clarke, summing up the Bullies' approach. "How can you skate if someone's on top of you and hitting you all the time?" One of

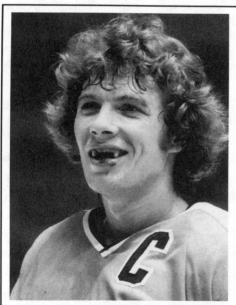

Bobby Clarke. "That tenacious gap-toothed rink rat, with the guts of ten dozen burglars."—*Mark Mulvoy.* Photo by Mel DiGiacomo/ Bruce Bennett Studios

the most telling incidents in Clarke's career came when he was playing for Team Canada in that historic 1972 meeting with the USSR, the first time stars from the NHL had played the Soviets in international competition. The heavily favored Canadian team was shocked in the opening games by the Russians led by the superb Valeriy Kharlamov. But Kharlamov later suffered an ankle injury, and the Canadians went on to take the last three games and win the series by the barest of margins. The absence of Kharlamov clearly hurt the Soviet team—a fact that Clarke, who delivered the slash that brought him down, was well aware of. "It's not something I'm really proud of," said Bobby. "But I can't say I was ashamed to do it."

How to Handle the Bullies

Those Flyers were tough, but they weren't unbeatable. Terry O'Reilly of the Boston Bruins knew how to handle them: Take names and numbers, and never give up. After being set upon by three Flyers during a game, O'Reilly fought back gamely, issuing this warning: "Guys, you can kill me. But you'd better go ahead and do it, because I know who you are, and I'll come back and take care of each of you in turn." Steven Seagal or Clint Eastwood couldn't have said it better.

Gretzky's Bodyguard

Dave Semenko was Wayne Gretzky's bodyguard on those great Edmonton Oiler teams of the eighties. "Far and away the greatest fighter I ever saw," recalls Gretzky. "He'd knock guys out with one punch and then hold them up so it didn't look so bad." Semenko had a great line: "Maybe you and I should go for a canoe ride"—he'd say this to a player on the opposing team, as a form of challenge, and as likely as not the player would skate off, unwilling to take the challenge.

Semenko was facing another big, tough guy, Kent "Killer"

Carlson, who stood 6-3 and weighed over 200. Semenko skated past him and said, "How'd you get your nickname, Killer? Shoot your dog?" But Killer didn't take the bait, and the two skated away, like two great sharks mutually deciding not to hunt the same waters.

ACE IS THE PLACE

Another former Gretzky bodyguard was Ace Bailey. They played together with Edmonton in the WHA. One game they were in, some guy was shadowing Gretzky all night long, and Gretzky just couldn't shake him. So Ace told Gretz, "Just bring him by the bench, I'll take care of him." The next time Gretzky got the puck he skated by the bench with the shadow right on his tail. But then suddenly the whistle blew, and the guy was out "colder than a popsicle," as Gretzky said. Ace had dropped him with his stick, but when everyone looked over to see what happened there was Ace, frantically pointing into the stands and shouting, "Do something, somebody! That guy up there threw something from the stands. Eject him!"

THE LAST MAN STANDING

Eddie Shore of the Boston Bruins was an irascible player and later, one of the orneriest hockey owners ever. When he played he was a terrific fighter, mean as a pit bull. He's in the Hockey Hall of Fame, but if he'd taken up boxing instead of hockey, he'd be in the Boxing Hall of Fame. "Shore jumped up and charged Bailey from behind, sending the Leaf player flying with a vicious check," writes Brian McFarlane, recreating a 1930s brawl involving Shore and Ace Bailey and Red Horner of the Leafs. "Bailey's head hit the ice with a crack. Red Horner of the Leafs retaliated at once. He smashed Shore in the face and knocked him out with one punch. Now there were two bodies on the ice, two heads oozing blood."

Shore would have fit in perfectly with the Big, Bad Bruins of the sixties and seventies. Then again, maybe he was too wild even for them. "When I was on the ice with my hockey stick," he told a teammate once, "I used it like a scientific tool; in your hands it's a blunt instrument." Here's another Eddie Shore fight, this one described by Stan Fischler: "Big, bruising Eddie Shore started the brawl by cross-checking minuscule Johnny Gagnon across the bridge of his nose with his stick. Minutes later Sylvio Mantha of the Canadiens clashed with Shore, and a bloody fight developed with referee Cooper Smeaton in the middle. The peace-maker Smeaton took three of Shore's hardest blows and fell to the ice with two broken ribs."

Shore was hockey's biggest drawing card in the 1920s. "What makes him that way is the hope entertained by spectators in all cities but Boston that he will some night be severely killed," writer Kyle Crichton explained. Besides his pugilistic abilities, what irritated non-Bostonians about Shore were his thespian qualities. On the ice he was a better actor than Olivier. "He could do a dying swan act that would have aroused the envy of Margot Fonteyn," cracked Baz O'Meara. Shore did these dying swan im-personations for the benefit of the referee, in the hopes that a penalty would be called on the player who whacked him.

Shore could give it, but more importantly, he could take it. That's one of the hallmarks of a true hockey tough guy. No one can win every fight, so what do you do when you lose one? You come back, that's what you do. "They broke his nose, slashed his face, and detached his teeth," said one newspaper account of an attack on Shore by several opponents. But always, always, Eddie Shore kept fighting, usually till no one was left standing but him.

KASPAR THE UNFRIENDLY GHOST

Darius Kasparaitis is an equal opportunity enforcer; he'll bash anybody. He doesn't even care if your name is Messier, Gretzky, or Hull. "It's no baby game," says Darius. "I'm in there to play tough, to hit people. I don't care who they are. Because you wear No. 66 you can't get hit? I don't believe that." As sportswriter Jeff Williams says, "If you're wearing the white, blue, and orange of the New York Islanders, Kasparaitis is great. If you're wearing any other, he grates on you."

The native-born Lithuanian— "Kaspar the unfriendly ghost," Williams calls him—grates on Islander foes, because he plays no favorites when it comes to bopping people. One hockey coach says that Darius is "so tough, it's scary." He tangled with the New Jersey Devils' Randy McKay, a hard guy himself, and knocked him out of the game. "He hurts people," said McKay. "He got me good. He saw his opportunity and he gave me a big hit. I definitely don't like the way he plays." Kasparaitis is a big-name hunter. The pelts on his wall include some of the biggest stars in hockey. A hard Kasparaitis check sent Brett Hull to the bench for three shifts. Darius creamed Eric Lindros in a scramble for the puck and the young Flyers star was jumping at his own shadow the rest of the game. Mark Messier has felt his wrath, as has Mario Lemieux. "I've never seen anyone hit the way Kaspar does," says an Islander teammate. "It's almost an art form the way he hits. I wouldn't want to be playing against him." Few people do.

"Here's Mud—er, Juice in Yer Eye!"

Paddy Moran played for the old Quebec Bulldogs in the early 1900s. His favorite technique for rattling opposing players was chopping at their skates. "Paddy was in a class by himself when it came to chopping the toes of opposing forwards," recalled Newsy Lalonde. "If he didn't disturb you that way, he'd spit tobacco juice in your eye."

Fighter Turned Broadcaster

Noel Picard was a fighter and a tough guy for the St. Louis Blues who, upon retiring from the game, found respectability in the TV

booth. Well, sort of. Once he was interviewing Philadelphia's Si-
mon Nolet, who had scrapped with Picard several times when
Noel was still lacing up the skates. "Simon," Noel asked in his
French Canadian accent, "in the early history of the Flyers and
Blues, there were a great many fights. How come?"

"You ought to know, Picard," Nolet responded. "You started
them all."

As a TV analyst, Picard was a great hockey player. He and an
announcer were doing the wrap-up at the end of a Blues game.
Noting that the Blues were about to embark on a three-game road
trip, the announcer asked Noel to talk about it. "Well, Dan," said
Picard, "the Blues have got a three-game road trip. They're gonna
go out and play three games, and then they're gonna come home."

THE BATTLING BROTHERS

Noel Picard played on the St. Louis Blues with Bob Plager and
John Arbor, both tough guys themselves. Brad Park said that playing against them was "like being a victim at a woodchopper's
ball." They cut and they slashed and they hacked. Bob had two
brothers, Barclay and Bill. The battling Plager brothers may have
been the fighting-est brother act in hockey history. Bob was
tough, but Barclay was tougher. Or maybe it was the other way
around. Playing on opposing NHL teams, they once got into it
against each other. But they disagreed afterwards on who won the
fight. "I licked him fair and square," said Bob from one locker
room. "The day that fat tub could get the better of me hasn't
come," responded Barclay from the other. And let's not forget the
youngest brother, Bill, who once broke Bob's hand in a fight. Just
be grateful you weren't *their* parents.

WILD BILL

Wild Bill Ezinicki played for the Toronto Maple Leafs in the late
1940s, and you didn't want to mess with him. His style, explained

one writer, was to take "a whack at everyone without bothering to examine their license plates." Ezinicki's body checks were ferocious. Here is how one Canadien player recalled a fierce body slam—uh, check—that Ezinicki threw on Montreal's Ken Reardon:

"Ezzie's shoulder caught Kenny squarely on the jaw. Kenny went down with a crash, rolled over, lurched unsteadily on his knees, then to his skates. His legs were so wobbly, he looked like he was giving one of those comic drunk routines. His eyes were actually crossed."

That was one Ezinicki hit, and there were many others that were equally punishing. The New York Rangers filed a complaint about one vicious Ezinicki hit, saying he was a dirty player. Toronto stuck behind its man, and offered to show the Rangers the film of the controversial hit. New York declined. Said Toronto's Conn Smythe: "They don't want to see a legal body check. It might give their players bad habits."

In Hockey Fights, 'Tis Better to Give

John Wesnick wore a Fu Manchu mustache and played hockey like one of Genghis Khan's marauders. He was a member of the Big, Bad Bruins under Don Cherry, and his former coach recalled him in action: "When he comes over the boards, he looks like he's stepping out of the pages of Horror Comics." Wesnick backed up his frightening visage with a pair of frightening fists. Just ask Keith Magnuson, former tough guy with the Chicago Blackhawks. Magnuson was no slouch himself; he never hesitated to face down a man if the situation called for it. "Sometimes somebody has to step into a guy, not necessarily in anger, but to set things right," he explained. Magnuson had only two rules when it came to fighting in hockey: Don't slug goalies and don't hit anyone with a wired jaw. After that, it was open season.

Magnuson and Wesnick crossed paths one day, and at least on this day, Magnuson came away a loser. Afterwards, in true tough-guy style, Wesnick mocked his beaten opponent: "I think Magnuson took lessons that it was better to receive than to give, because he received one punch after another."

HIGH-STICKING LEO

Leo Labine played for the Boston Bruins in the 1950s, and he was known for putting his stick in the faces of opposing players. Opposing players did not like this, but Leo cared not a whit. "I don't know anybody who likes to eat wood," said Leo, "unless he's a beaver." Once Leo put his stick in the face of the temperamental Rocket Richard, who retaliated by placing his stick in Leo's chops. Leo, in turn, did not respond kindly. "Look Rocket," he said, "you've got thirty-two teeth. Do you want to try for sixteen?"

Late in his career the older and wiser Labine mellowed somewhat, frowning on the stick-in-your-face tactics that characterized his youth. After a Maple Leaf player broke a stick over his head, Leo, aghast, said, "You shouldn't do that. You'll get a penalty." In like a lion, Leo went out like a lamb.

TWO MORE STICKHANDLERS

Two more guys who knew how to handle a stick were Ken Reardon of the Canadiens and Bobby Schmautz of the Bruins. "If Schmautz carried his stick any higher," said the columnist Mike Barnicle, "someone in the third deck could have reached out and stolen it." Then there was the time Reardon was skating along the boards and a fan yelled at him, "You're a brave man with a hockey stick in your hands." Reardon promptly hit the fan over his head with his stick.

BIG, BAD BRUINS

The Big, Bad Bruins were to hockey in the late sixties and early seventies what the Broad Street Bullies were in the late seventies and eighties. They were a vastly talented team that included

Bobby Orr, Phil Esposito, and Gerry Cheevers, but they also had some real "animals." That was another name for these Boston teams: "the Animals." Here are brief looks at a few of the Animals:

A Teacher of Youth

Johnny McKenzie, said former NHL referee Bruce Hood, was "reckless, a guy who just didn't give a damn. He'd fly into those corners at full speed, arms and elbows flying, and come out with the puck on his stick and a grin on his face." One time Johnny was speaking to a group of schoolchildren. One child in the assembly held up his hand and asked what McKenzie did when he saw someone coming down the ice to fight him. "I reach back and take what I can find in the back of my hockey pants and I throw it at the guy," Johnny said, smiling.

The Intimidator

Wayne Cashman was one of the most intimidating Bruins but unlike McKenzie, he was not a Bruce Hood favorite. "Nobody played the intimidation role better," said Hood. "He made sure everyone knew that if you messed with him, you messed with all the Bruins. He liked that power and took advantage of it. When a guy was down," Hood adds, "Cashman always looked ready to kick him." Cashman intimidated referees just as he intimidated players. Hood recalls Cashman standing about three feet away from him holding his stick out, examining the blade like a person sharpening a knife. "I'd like to gouge somebody's eyes out with this stick," Cashman said, making sure Hood heard him and knew whom he was referring to. In all his years in the NHL, including playing for Team Canada in the 1972 series with the Soviet Union, Cashman did not, however, ever gouge anyone's eyes out with a stick.

Terrible Ted

"Terrible Ted" Green was the baddest dude on those Bruins, one of the meanest of all hockey fighters, and he suffered a terrible price for it. In a September 1969 incident, Wayne Maki of St. Louis cracked him in the head with a hockey stick and fractured his skull, partially paralyzing him. Doctors put a plate in his head, and he later resumed his NHL career. "What's the matter Greenie," fans would shout at him if he started faltering, "that plate in your head too heavy for you?"

That may seem cruel, but in his prime Terrible Ted was merciless toward his opponents. He protected Bobby Orr and Phil Esposito on the Bruins and he did it with all the subtlety of a Mafia hitman. Brad Park of the New York Rangers called him a hatchet man, remembering this incident: "We had the puck in Boston's end of the rink. Vic Hadfield took a shot at the goal, and the puck went past Green's head. Right away, Green got the idea that Hadfield shot at him. So what does Green do? As Vic skated away he swung his stick with both hands and cracked Hadfield across the small of the back, sending Vic down for the count." Park adds, "That's what I mean by a hatchet man—one who'll swing his stick at anybody."

SAVED BY A NOSE

When you talk about Montreal Canadien tough guys, one name pops to the top of the list: John Ferguson. "I made sure I was the meanest bastard who ever went in the corners for a puck," Ferguson said, and if he wasn't, he was awfully close.

"John Ferguson scared the wits out of me," said referee Bruce Hood. "He looked and acted like he was always a step away from exploding, and that's what scared me. I always figured if he ever snapped, he'd go right through the end boards and take someone with him." The tightly coiled Ferguson didn't fight as much as some other hockey tough guys; no need. "One look into his eyes was usually enough to warn opposing players not to mess with him," said Hood.

"He's the type of player who likes to run right over you," said Brad Park. But one time Ferguson tried to run over Park, and the Rangers defenseman threw a hip check on him that sent him sprawling. "He landed on his head and shoulder," Park recalled, adding that luckily the fall didn't do any damage to one of Ferguson's most intimidating physical characteristics: his nose. "Fortunately it wasn't his nose [that got hit], because if that nose gets any bigger, he'll have a difficult time finding the rink," said Park.

MELONHEAD

One reporter sniffed that bad guy Tie Domi's "hockey gifts are limited to punching." Okay, so what's wrong with that? One thing's for sure: the reporter didn't make this remark to Tie personally. Otherwise, well, you know—Tie might have rearranged the reporter's face. Last seen throwing his body around for the Winnipeg Jets, Tie is one of the baddest dudes in the NHL. He carries a grudge the way hockey players carry sticks. A few years ago, when he was with the Rangers, Tie refused to shake Claude Lemieux's hand after a playoff series. "The guy called me a melonhead," said Tie, who really does look like a Casaba. "Why should I shake his hand? If I shake his hand, that means I'm his friend. I never have to be nice to him. He's a jughead."

ROCKET'S NEMESIS

Ted Lindsay had a simple philosophy: "I hate everyone on the opposition." Lindsay played with Gordie Howe in the 1950s and hated everyone who wasn't a Detroit Red Wing. Lindsay—like Ted Green, nicknamed "Terrible Ted" for his ferocious style of play—was feared by many in the NHL, though Montreal's Frank Selke, Sr. wasn't one of them. "I interpret toughness with ability to back up any situation which may arise," said Selke. "I cannot place Lindsay in this category, because he is mean and quick with his skates but cannot back it up with his dukes." Lindsay had a thing against Montreal— "I'd play the Canadiens for nothing, just to get a good piece of them," he said—and he took it out on Rocket

Richard whenever they played. The Hall of Famer Richard rated the Hall of Famer Lindsay as his toughest foe. "For me," said Richard, "the worst player by far whom I ever skated against was Ted Lindsay. He had a dirty mouth. He swore at everybody on the ice." Lindsay skated hard and cursed and skated hard and cursed and skated hard some more. His campaign to defuse the Rocket was unrelenting. Why, even his wife got into the act. Richard continues, "He was a bad man with everything—his mouth, his stick—and off the ice, it was the same thing. Even his wife would yell and swear at me."

"WENDY" NO MORE

Some people used to rag on Wendel Clark. They said that while he may have been a tiger when his team played at home, on the road he was a pussycat. "He's Wendel at home and Wendy on the road," went the rap against him. Not so anymore. Jeff Norton, among many others, will vouch for that. Clark put on a hit on Norton during a 1994 Leafs-Sharks playoff game that, as Austin Murphy said, "bent [Norton] into a horseshoe." Murphy writes, "So enthusiastically did Clark finish his check that Norton was left gazing up into his teammates' nostrils." His teammates helped the dazed and semiconscious Norton off the ice. Another playoff victim that year was Chicago's Chris Chelios, who was knocked silly by a Clark check.

Clark doesn't go to blows as much as he used to, but "he can still fight like a bastard," said Toronto's Bill Waters. Todd Gill, a former teammate of Clark's on the Leafs, adds, "There's not a guy in the league that wants a piece of him. Wendel isn't swinging for show. He's swinging to hurt you." Wendel's hockey philosophy stems from his father, Les, a Saskatchewan wheat farmer. "Dad always said, 'I don't care what you do, just do it as hard as you can,'" recalls his son, who puts that philosophy into practice every time he laces on the skates.

OTHER TOUGH GUYS WE HAVE KNOWN

By his own estimate, Sprague Cleghorn participated in fifty "stretcher-case fights." Sprague had a fifteen-year career, which makes for more than three fights per season. . . . Clark Gillies of the New York Islanders not only physically intimidated the opposition, he threatened to eat them. An opposing defenseman was bullying one of Gillies's teammates and Clark skated up to him and said, "You touch him and I'll eat you for lunch." Not wanting to be an appetizer, the defenseman skated away.

Jerry "King Kong" Korab's philosophy of hockey was to mix it up. "I don't feel like I'm in the game unless somebody takes me into the boards or I take someone else for a ride," he said. "If the game gets quiet, I find it sort of boring." The game seldom got boring with big Jerry around. . . . Walter Tkaczuk was a strongman for the New York Rangers. One off-season he decided to go into the gym and build his body up some more. "That's like a Sherman tank adding a bulldozer," said a teammate in awe. . . . Blake Ball, Don Perry, and John Brophy terrorized the old Eastern League. "With these guys as competition," cracked broadcaster Gene Hart, "Attila the Hun would have won the Lady Byng Trophy." . . . Did anybody have anything good to say about Red Wings toughie Tony Leswick? "I have nothing good to say about Tony Leswick," said Rocket Richard. Oh.

The reason a lot of hockey players play tough is simple: They need to in order to survive in the game. "There's no getting around it," said Steve Durbano, one-time hockey bad guy. "I'm dirty. I admit it. I have to be. I'm trying to make a name for myself. Any name." . . . Sometimes, though, when you go looking for trouble, you'll find it. In the 1950s Bill Juzda was a tough-talking baddie for the Maple Leafs. In one Leaf-Canadien alley fight he said something off-color to Rocket Richard, who hauled off and popped him one. "I reared back—and *foom!*—I hit him a good one and he went down flat on his back," recalled Richard. "Poor Juzda was out cold. But he deserved it. He was one of those typical NHL bullies who thought he could push everybody around without retaliation." Not so, at least not with the Rocket around.

In 1994 the *Hockey News* designated Pittsburgh's Rick Tocchet as "the most dangerous forward" in hockey, based on a formula that included points scored and penalty minutes. Tocchet received a one-year subscription to the magazine to be sent to the Civic Arena penalty box. . . . Don Cherry is a big fan of Red Wing enforcer Bob Probert. In his rap video Cherry sang: "Probert, Probert, what a man; we see him, it's slam bam." Not exactly Snoop Doggy Dogg, Don. Work on it. . . . When you tangled with Newsy Lalonde in the old days, it was bad news. "Lalonde could buckle a swash with any ruffian alive," wrote Dick Beddoes. A more vivid description of Newsy's pugilistic exploits came from an unknown source: "Lalonde spilled enough corpuscles to gratify any blood bank on the continent."

Hockey legend Maurice "Rocket" Richard was a great player and a pretty tough customer. He had to be. As the writer Bill Roche says, "Maurice should know a lot about the sour science of pro wrestling, for he has had nearly all the headlocks, scissor holds and other grips and grabs applied on him. Further, if all the high sticks that have been thrust at his head were laid end to end, he'd have quite a flourishing lumberyard." . . . Yessiree, Eddie Shack of the Boston Bruins could handle himself pretty well in a fight. But like all good fighters, he learned to pick his spots. After a stick-swinging fight with Larry Zeidel, Shack said he was backing off: "I play hockey to score goals, not fight the village idiot."

6

DON CHERRY SPEAKS! (AND SPEAKS! AND SPEAKS!)

Don Cherry, says the columnist Trent Frayne, is "the most refreshing, ungrammatical, opinionated, entertaining, funny, outrageous, exhilarating, and occasionally boring commentator" on television. For those Americans who may not be aware of Cherry's unique charms, he is comparable in some ways to Howard Cosell, although, thankfully, without Cosell's boring pomposity. Cherry, like Cosell in his glory days, is a story unto himself, often dwarfing the games and players he is covering by his personality and celebrity status. Like Cosell, Cherry's opinions can be hard to take at times, but he is impossible to ignore and almost always lots of fun.

ON FIGHTING

Don Cherry is the game's leading advocate of fighting. He likes it and thinks it should remain part of the game. When Edmonton coach and GM Glen Sather spoke out against showing fights on TV, Cherry called him "a two-faced hypocrite." In the 1980s, when the Oilers were winning all those Stanley Cups with Wayne Gretzky, they had one of the toughest teams in the league, in large part to protect the Great One. Said Cherry: "If you even touched Gretzky or looked sideways at him, you'd have five guys beating you up. Now that he [Sather] doesn't have a tough team, he doesn't want fighting in the league."

ON FIGHTING, AND THE EUROPEAN STYLE OF HOCKEY

Cherry can't stand the European style of hockey. The Europeans pussyfoot around too much, he says; passing and skating and passing and skating and would somebody please take a shot? Cherry is an advocate of the North American style, which, if it sometimes resembles a mugging on skates, who cares? At least it's our Canadian boys who are doing the mugging. Here is what he says to people who want to ban fighting from hockey: "The fans love fighting. The players don't mind. The coaches like the fights. What's the big deal? The players who don't want to fight don't have to fight. Do you ever see Wayne Gretzky in a fight? What's the big deal? I saw Winnipeg and New Jersey the other night, and they were just skating around, skating around. It was like a tea party, like watching Sweden and Finland play."

ONE DRAWBACK OF FIGHTING

Don Cherry is not wholly in favor of fighting, understand. There are some drawbacks to it. As he says, "The worst feeling in the world is when your thumb gets caught in the other guy's mouth."

ON THE RUSSIAN INVASION

Cherry doesn't like Russian players any more than he does the Europeans. After nine Russians claimed roster spots in the NHL for the 1989–90 season, he said: "I know what it's like to have somebody take your job. And listen, when a Russian gets $700,000 to play hockey here, $350,000 goes to the Russian federation to make their hockey players better. It's like Wayne Gretzky says, nobody ever gave *his* folks anything."

ON THE INFLUENCE OF EUROPEANS ON THE NHL

Cherry's critics say that he's xenophobic, which is a fancy way of saying he hates non-Canadians. That may be overly harsh, but one thing is for sure: he should not apply to become an ambassador to the United Nations. Here is what he said about the influence of foreign players on the NHL: "They talk about all the things the foreign players have brought to the game. Well, let's see, what have they brought? The helmet. The visor. The dive. Lying there and letting on that you're hurt, the way soccer players always do. I guess, you look at it that way, these people are right. The foreign players have brought a lot into the game."

ON WHY NHL PLAYERS ARE GETTING SO WIMPY

The NHL is a lot wimpier than it used to be, and in Cherry's mind this is in part due to the arrival of European players like Jaromir Jagr. "It used to be, you'd get cut, you'd finish your shift, no matter what," Cherry says. "A guy like Tim Horton of Toronto, the blood would be coming down his face, and he'd finish his shift. You'd want to get up there to the NHL to be like Tim Horton. Now you have a guy like Jaromir Jagr of the Penguins. Jaromir Jagr is everything that's wrong with the NHL. He gets hit, he goes down and stays there. Get up!'"

ON THE FISHING WARS

In 1990, the Canadian fishing industry was under intense competition from foreign fishermen. The foreigners, said the Canadians, were overfishing the waters of the Maritime provinces and putting Canadian fishermen out of work. The Canadian government was even trying to get the foreign fleets to leave, or at least reduce the amount of their catch.

About the same time, at the world junior hockey championships in Sweden, a kid named Norris scored the game-winning goal against the Soviet Union, earning Canada the gold medal. Norris hailed from Newfoundland, one of the provinces most affected by the fishing controversy. When Don Cherry heard about this, he exulted on the air, saying, "And how about that Norris kid from Newfoundland, is he something else? Way to go from the Rock! I know they don't like to call it the Rock but I call it the Rock anyhow. He said, you know, here's what he said, 'You steal our money on the tours, you steal our fish, you steal our fishing, you foreigners, but you can't steal the gold!' Way to go!"

At which point broadcast partner Ron MacLean interjected, "This is a new area of expertise, I guess."

To which Cherry responded: "Yeah, and I'll tell you one thing down there—I would like to be the commissioner of fisheries. I'll tell you, no foreign boat would take one of our fish. That's what I'd like to do. You guys, eh? Norris, you've got the hockey straightened out. Straighten out those guys in the fish!"

On Tomas Sandstrom

Whatever you think about Don Cherry, he is nothing if not blunt. He calls a Swede a Swede. This is what he had to say about Kings forward Tomas Sandstrom: "Tomas Sandstrom. A lot of people think he is Little Lord Fauntleroy, but Tomas Sandstrom is a backstabbing, cheap-shot, mask-wearing Swede." And this is what Cherry said about him *on the air*. Imagine what Cherry says about Sandstrom in private.

Going to the Dogs

Don Cherry is also no big fan of Alpo Suhonen (who, not coincidentally, is no fan of his). When the Winnipeg Jets hired the

Finnish Suhonen to coach a minor league farm team, Cherry cracked, "Alpo? That's a dog food isn't it?"

DON MAKES A MISTAKE (AND ALMOST ADMITS IT)

Sometimes even Don Cherry makes a mistake. And if you back him up against a wall with a firing squad pointed at him, maybe— just maybe—he will admit to it. Early in the 1993–94 season Cherry had unkind things to say about Sergei Makarov, the one-time Russian great who had struggled in the NHL. Makarov, said Cherry, "wouldn't score 27 goals in a season if he lived to be a hundred." As it happened Makarov went on to score 30 goals for the San Jose Sharks that season. Asked about his earlier comment, Cherry said, "He got 30, eh? Shows you where the league is going."

Cherry went on, "It looks like he [Makarov] is having fun again. That's a big thing with the Europeans—if they're having fun, they play. I think mostly they're magicians; they disappear in the play-offs. But the league has turned into a Nolan Ryan league: no hits. Those guys are all protected. I'd like to take that team [the Sharks] into Philadelphia back in 1978."

DON'S PLAYING CAREER

Now, this won't take long . . . For a guy who knows so much, Cherry didn't exactly have a storied NHL playing career. He played one game—count it, one game—in the NHL. The rest of his sixteen hockey-playing years were spent in the minors, bouncing from Palookaville to Podunk and points in between. In 1962, Montreal acquired the pugnacious defenseman for its farm system. How much did it pay? "Two rolls of tape and a jockstrap," says Don, and the jockstrap was used.

On Hockey in the South

After retiring from the game, Cherry coached a number of teams that were not very good. This was hard on his psyche. "It's tough to fly like an eagle when you're surrounded by turkeys," he explains. Nonetheless he plugged on, determined to stay in the game even though nobody seemed to want him. There was a time in Cherry's career when he was wandering the hockey wasteland looking for a job. No one would hire him. He even went to Charlotte, North Carolina, hoping to land a position there. But he immediately had second thoughts. "I went down to Charlotte for an interview and some Southerner says, 'What's your philosophy on hockey?' What the fuck was I doing sitting there trying to talk philosophy with some guy from Charlotte?"

On Coaching the Bruins

Finally, Cherry got the job of his life coaching the Boston Bruins. Cherry coached the Bruins for five years. They were the Big, Bad Bruins with stars like Bobby Orr and Phil Esposito, and Cherry loved that team. Here's one of his fondest memories from those years: "I don't think any team had more fun than that one. I remember one night we're playing LA, and Hilliard Graves hits Bobby Orr from behind. I went crazy. I grab a guy, Hank Nowak, and send him over the boards screaming, 'Get him, Get him, Get him.' Poor Nowak, he skates to the blue line and turns around. 'Get who?' he asks."

The Bruins vs. the Flyers

Cherry's Bruins and the Philadelphia Flyers were the two most physical teams of that era. Physical? Okay, they bashed one another's brains out whenever they played. Except for their respective fans, few in the NHL liked either the Bruins or the

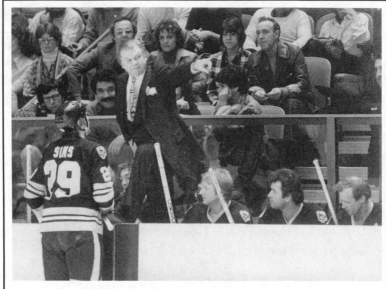

Don Cherry when he was coaching the Boston Bruins. Photo by Bruce Bennett

Flyers, and that includes the officials who called their games. The referees, in fact, gave both teams a very wide berth—and Cherry thought he knew why. "I know why the referees don't call many penalties when the Bruins and Flyers are playing," he said. "Either they're hoping they kill each other, or they can't figure out which team they hate the most."

On Fathering Mike Milbury's Child

One of the Bruins he didn't like from those days, however, was Dallas Smith. Recalled Cherry: "Dallas Smith, he was so much smarter than me and he's looking at me like, Who is this dumdum? I was the only guy in the world who didn't like Dallas Smith." Mike Milbury was a different story. Cherry loved Milbury like a son and Milbury loved Cherry like a father. In fact, in a radio interview after the birth of his first child, Milbury said, "I think so much of Don Cherry that I made him the father of my

child." Mike meant to say "godfather," but his teammates heard
the blooper and never let him forget it.

TROUBLE WITH HARRY

Harry Sinden was Cherry's GM at Boston, and a famous penny-
pincher. The two men once argued publicly over some Czecho-
slovakian-made pucks that Sinden, as an economy move, had
purchased for the Bruins. They may not have been great pucks,
but they did produce a couple of great Cherry one-liners. "Those
pucks are so cheap, when they go in the stands the fans fire them
back at us," said Cherry. He added, "No rookie wants to score his
first goal in Boston, because they don't want a cheap Czechoslo-
vakian puck on their mantel."

ON CONSULTING PIECES OF PAPER

Don Cherry doesn't like coaches who consult pieces of paper
behind the bench. As a matter of fact, when he was a player,
he used to laugh at them. "We used to sit there and wonder,
'Doesn't this guy know what lines we have? Doesn't he know
the team?'"

ON BEING SO OUTSPOKEN

While coach of the Bruins, Cherry got PO'ed at Chicago's Stan
Mikita, threatening to have his players "send him back to Czecho-
slovakia in a pine box." Cherry also said that overweight Bruin
winger Rick Middleton "looked like Porky the Pig." Such plain-
spokenness has of course been a trademark of his broadcasting
career. He demanded on the air that someone break the Pittsburgh defenseman Ulf Samuelsson's arm "between the wrist and
the elbow." In a rare moment of introspection, Cherry said to a
reporter, "I can't keep saying these things. How can I keep saying these things?" But he does.

ON WOMEN TALKING AT HOCKEY GAMES

Don Cherry is not what you'd call "politically correct." After a woman got hit in the face with a hockey puck at a game he was attending, he weighed in with these words: "I was watching from the stands in the first period. There was a tipped shot, and I had to get out of the way, and it went over my head and hit this poor lady in the face. I'm telling you, when you come to the game, ladies, keep your eye on the puck. I've seen some awful smacks, and it's always a woman, just talking away, not paying any attention."

ON BECOMING AN AUTHOR

Like a lot of famous people, Don Cherry has written his autobiography. Well, actually, like a lot of famous people, his publisher paid someone to write an autobiography for him. Reflecting on how a person with such rotten grammar could come to write a book, Cherry said: "Three years ago I couldn't *spell* 'author.' Now I *are* one."

ON BROADCASTING IN MONTREAL

Cherry's broadcast partner at CBC, Ron MacLean, tells about an incident in which they were taping a show in Montreal. Says MacLean: "We're at the studio. Don likes to arrive late. He likes everything to be spontaneous. I'm doing some work, and I notice the director is speaking in French. He's counting down, *'dix, neuf, huit, sept . . .* ' Okay, we're in a place where the people speak French. Their language. No problem. Don comes in. The director starts the same thing. Cherry goes crazy. 'What is this *einzfreinz* crap? English! This is a program in English!' The director begins again: 'Ten, nine, eight . . . '"

ON EXPANSION

Like many hockey traditionalists, Cherry is not thrilled by expansion. Too many teams dilute the quality of play. As he said a few years ago: "The NHL is expanding to Anaheim and Miami. Disney is in Anaheim, and the video guy [Wayne Huizenga, owner of Blockbuster Video and the Florida Panthers] is in Miami. Okay, two heavy hitters like that come knocking, you'd better open the door. But tell me this, where are they going to get the players? Would you mind telling me? You already got Ottawa. Ottawa! Tampa Bay, San Jose, sinking fast. Where are they going to get the players?"

ON CHANGING THE GAME OF HOCKEY

Don Cherry is suspicious of hockey Johnny-come-latelies who want to change the game to make it more palatable for the masses. A few of these people even occupy powerful positions in the NHL. Cherry points out that an interim NHL president "never saw a hockey game until he was thirty-nine years old." Cherry adds that many of these newcomers "wouldn't know a hockey player if they slept with Bobby Orr." Cherry says, "They all want to change something. They think if they change—if they take out the fights, do something different—hockey is going to become big in the U.S. The big TV contract. It just isn't going to happen. Face it, people in the U.S. would rather watch *The Rifleman* than a hockey game. It's almost sad the way our people try to market this game. Let it stand for itself. Let it be what it is."

SOUR ON GRAPES

Not everyone is a fan of Don Cherry's. Come to think of it, a lot of people find him hard to stomach. Here are a few voices from the anti-Cherry contingent:

"Mouthy people like the Big Italian always find a job some-where in hockey. It's Don Cherry who should be looking over his shoulder. Hockey Night in Canada *could easily find a big mouth capable of shouting louder and making more outrageous state-ments per minute than him."*

> —Columnist Rejean Tremblay, taking a shot at Cherry on the occasion of Phil Es-posito's firing as GM and coach of the Rangers

"Between you and me, I think Don Cherry has been standing next to the speakers at an Aerosmith concert. His brain's a little rattled."

> —Ann Killion, sports columnist

"Cherry's jingoistic fervor makes Rush Limbaugh look like a card-carrying member of the Communist Party."

> —Anthony Reilly, magazine writer

"I think Don is very predictable. I think he's fun, but he's al-ways been who he is. I guess he likes goon hockey. Well, the pub-lic doesn't, and the league doesn't, and the people running the game don't."

> —Gil Stein, NHL executive

"Don Cherry is like Humphrey Bogart in the wrong movie. He's real, but he doesn't fit in all the different situations he's in."

> —Alpo Suhonen, Winnipeg assistant coach

"He's a total idiot. He's a goof. I ignore him. He accuses all Eu-ropean players of not playing physically, but not all Canadian and U.S. players have the same skills as the Europeans. You can't crit-icize these players for not fighting, because they never did it back

*home. If they grew up here, maybe they would be more willing to
do that. What can you say? He's a goof."*

—Frank Musil, Czech-born defenseman

FRACTURED ENGLISH

Somebody once described Don Cherry as "hockey's Dizzy Dean,"
referring to the former baseball pitcher who became a TV broadcaster and irritated English teachers across America with his
folksy sayings and fractured syntax. Cherry is much the same. He
drops his g's—nothin' and somethin', for instance—and says
what's on his mind, even if it comes out sounding a little . . . odd.
"You know we have a language policy here," said a broadcast executive, protesting the decision to hire Cherry on *Hockey Night
in Canada*. "This guy doesn't speak English." This executive
couldn't have foreseen that Cherry would be a hit in part because
of his unusual way with words. As Ralph Mellanby, former
Hockey Night in Canada producer, points out, "Don has become
a TV star in two languages—and he doesn't speak either of them."

How Don Cherry Got His Break in Broadcasting

Ralph Mellanby was the man who tabbed Don Cherry for *Hockey
Night in Canada*. Then executive producer of the show, Mellanby
told *Sports Illustrated* how the Boston coach first barged into his
consciousness:

"I met him when he was in his last year as coach of the Bruins. That was when I first started thinking about him for TV. The
Bruins were playing the Canadiens in the semifinals. He was
coaching, and I was producing the games. After the second game
he came up to me all mad. There had been a fight. Stan Jonathan
of Boston had beaten up someone from Montreal. Cherry had
seen a tape of the game and saw that we hadn't replayed the fight.
He wanted to know if it was because a Bruin had won the fight.
I told him it was our practice; we didn't replay fights."

Mellanby continues, "During the fourth game there was another fight. This was at the Montreal Forum. Mario Tremblay won
the fight. He beat up someone from the Bruins. We're doing the
game from this little production room at the Forum and suddenly
we can see on one of the monitors that Cherry isn't behind the
bench anymore. Where'd he go? This looks like it might be a
story. Suddenly he's in the production room. In the middle of a
Stanley Cup game. He's talking to me, telling that we'd better not
replay this fight either. He was worried because a Montreal guy
had won. I remember thinking, The middle of a game. This guy
is interesting."

ON GOLF

Don Cherry on golf: "Who would want to be a golfer? You me-
ander along after a ball. No one hits it to you."

ON PASSING VERSUS SCORING GOALS

Don Cherry believes in selfless hockey play, passing to your teammates rather than hogging the puck and shooting yourself. Well,
maybe not. Some time ago Cherry was watching one of his friend's
kids play hockey, a twenty-year-old named Todd. On a breakaway
Todd juked out the goalie but rather than shoot the puck himself,
slid it over to his teammate, who shot it into the net. Afterwards a
concerned Cherry took Todd aside. "Listen, kid," he said, "I'm
gonna tell you something. The guys that score goals in hockey are
the ones that everybody hears about. Those guys that score goals,
lots of goals, they're the ones that drive Cadillacs."

Todd continued to listen, while Cherry continued to impart his
hard-won advice: "The guys that pass them the puck to let them
score goals, kid, they're the guys that drive Volkswagens. Now
think about it, kid. What do you want to drive when you grow
up?"

"I'd like a motorcycle," said Todd.

On His Dog, Blue

When Don Cherry was coaching the Bruins, his dog, Blue, became almost as famous as Cherry himself. Blue was an English
bullterrier who starred in her own commercials and figured
prominently in many of her master's yarns. Then Blue bit Rose,
Don's wife, and it was a sad day in the Cherry household. "You're
going to have to get rid of her," a friend told Don. "I know," said
Cherry. "Me and Blue will really miss her."

On His Broadcasting Style

Don Cherry explains his broadcasting style: "I react, I can't re-
hearse. If I have to say something twice it's no good. One time,
at Rochester, I'm playing for Joe Crozier and I go, 'Joe, I think
that . . .' And Joe interrupts and goes, 'Grapes, don't think. You'll
hurt the hockey club.'" So remember, Don: Never, never think.
We're all enjoying it too much.

7

GOALIES

Goalies don't get into many fights, but they sure are tough. You have to be tough to stand down a puck coming at you at 100 mph. Goalies can also be a bit on the flaky side. They're a part of the team, and yet they're not a part. Their role is unlike any other player. Their unique position tends to make them look at life—and hockey—a little bit differently than anyone else. This chapter is devoted to goalies, past and present, who step to the beat of a different drummer.

GOALIES TALK ABOUT GOALTENDING

One of the greatest-ever goalies, Jacques Plante, said, "Only a goalie can appreciate what a goalie goes through." With that in mind, here are the thoughts of goalies on their noble craft:

> *"There is no position in sport as noble as goaltending."*
> —Vladislav Tretiak, the great Russian goalie

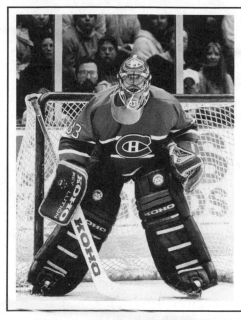

Patrick Roy, Montreal Canadiens. "There is no position in sport as noble as goaltending."—*Vladislav Tretiak.* Photo by John Giamundo/Bruce Bennett Studios

"Playing goal is like being shot at."
                                    —Jacques Plante

"The goalie is like the guy on the minefield. He discovers the mines and destroys them. If you make a mistake, somebody gets blown up."
                                    —Arturs Irbe, San Jose Sharks goalie

"We are the sort of people who make health insurance popular."
                                    —Hall of Fame goalie Terry Sawchuk, on
                                    the oft-injured state of goalies

"In Biblical times I stoned people to death. Now they are re-paying me by hurling pucks at my head."
                                    —Giles Gratton, former goaltender with
                                    somewhat mystical bent

"Grim, humorless, largely uncreative, getting little physical pleasure in return."
—Ken Dryden, retired Montreal goalie

"It's the only way I can support my family. If I could do it some other way, I wouldn't be playing goal."
—Glenn Hall, Hall of Fame goalie

A Former Heavyweight Boxing Champion Talks about Why He'd Never Be a Goalie

"I don't want nothing comin' at me that I can't stop."
—Joe Frazier

A Goalie's Life

For a goalie, said the great Glenn Hall, a hockey game is "sixty minutes of hell." Being a goaltender in a hockey game is unlike any other position in sports, except perhaps for javelin catcher. Javelin catching, of course, was banned from Olympic competition due to too many injuries. Here are some more thoughts on playing goal and the men who do it:

"Any discussion on hockey goaltenders must begin with the assumption that they are about three sandwiches shy of a picnic. I can prove this. From the moment Primitive Man first lurched erect, he and those who came after him survived on the principle that when something hard and potentially painful comes at you at great velocity, you get the hell out of its path. Goalkeepers throw themselves into its path. I rest my case."
—Jim Taylor, columnist

"A goalie just stands there, seemingly impassive but actually boiling inside. They play a different game than anyone else. The closest approach in another sport might be the catcher in baseball. But still, he does things that are baseball—goes up to hit, chases

fouls, etc. In hockey, a goalie does nothing that other players do. Except for his sweater, he even dresses differently right down to his skates."
—Muzz Patrick, old-time coach

"How many people in life spend eighteen years getting shot at?"
—Kevin Constantine, hockey coach

"Goalies are fine fellows when you meet them at center ice. They are fine fellows off the ice too. But don't think this cordiality is going to apply when you skate by the front of his cave. He'll slice you up if you come in close."
—Chandler Sterling, writer

"There is no such thing as painless goaltending. If they could get enough padding to assure against every type of bruise, you'd have to be swung into position with a small derrick."
—Don Cherry

"You put on years when you put on a goaltender's equipment. A twenty-year-old kid is suddenly middle-aged when he's got that stuff on."
—Ted Green, former NHL star

"Goaltending is a suffering position. Your equipment protects you from injury, but not from pain, every time you go out there. And if you allow a goal, the red lights go on for everyone to see. But you get to be a hero too."
—Kevin Constantine

DONNING THE MASK

Jacques Plante might be considered the first modern goalie. He did not invent the goalie mask, nor was he was the first to use one in competition (that honor belongs to Clint Benedict). But Plante made it respectable. Now it's a commonplace. A goalie would be considered nuts if he went onto the ice without a mask. In Plante's day, he was considered nuts because he did.

Benedict, the first to wear a mask, did so after being struck in the face by a Howie Morenz shot in a 1930 game. Twenty-nine years later a similar incident made Plante, in 1959, seek protection. For him it was an Andy Bathgate missile to the face during a game against the Rangers. Plante retreated to the Canadiens' locker room and told his coach, Toe Blake, that he wasn't going back onto the ice without something to protect his face. Blake said yes, and history was made.

The Bathgate incident was the last straw for Plante—or more exactly, the last stitch. He was sick and tired of getting beaten up and stitched up. "I already had four broken noses, a broken jaw, two broken cheekbones, and almost two-hundred stitches in my head," said Plante. "I didn't care how the mask looked. I was afraid I would look just like the mask, the way things were going." Fans all over the league razzed Plante for his strange get-up— "Hey Plante, Halloween's over," they yelled—and reporters quizzed him about his courage. "Doesn't the fact you're wearing a mask prove you're afraid?" one reporter asked. "If you jumped out of a plane without a parachute," Plante calmly replied, "would that prove you're brave?" It would, of course, prove something quite different, and now every goaltender agrees with Plante. As Patrick Roy of Montreal says, "The scariest thing in the world is losing your mask." But before Jacques Plante, every goalie faced that kind of fear.

GUMP

Gump Worsley, who played for Plante's Canadiens and the New York Rangers, was one of the last goalies not to wear a mask. "Anybody who wears a mask is scared," he said. Well, that was Gump for you. He was "his ownself," to borrow Dan Jenkins's term. Reporters got out their thesauruses to find new and different ways to describe Gump the Lump, who was 5-6 and fat as a teddy bear.

Rotund was very popular. More original was George Plimpton: "Turnip-shaped," he called him. Best of all was the sportswriter who likened Gump to "a badly packed Army duffel bag."

Gump was once asked what team gave him the most trouble as a goalie. "The Rangers," answered Gump. Gump was playing for the Rangers at the time. Because of his less than impressive physique, Gump did not see eye to eye with his coach on the Rangers, Phil Watson, and they frequently went belly-to-belly on the subject. "How can we win when our goalie has a beer belly?" said Watson. Said Gump: "It just goes to show you what a dope we have for a coach. Everyone knows I don't drink beer, just Johnny Walker Red."

THE FAT MAN

Turk Broda was an all-time great goalie for the Maple Leafs, although, like Gump Worsley and some other goalies, he was a fatty. "The oldest, fattest, baldest, and best goalkeeper" in professional hockey in the 1940s, was how sportswriter Trent Frayne described him. In a famous 1949 incident, Conn Smythe, the Toronto owner, issued a public challenge to Broda to shed some pounds. "My goalie's too fat," said Smythe. "He'd better lose seven pounds before the next game or I'll be looking for another goalie." Smythe added, "We are not running a fat man's team." Turk lost the weight and played the next game, throwing a zero at the New York Rangers.

A NEW GOALTENDING TECHNIQUE

Steve Buzinski was known as "the Human Sieve," and for good reason. He played goaltender for the New York Rangers during World War II, when the domestic shortage of able-bodied men forced hockey teams to sign players who ordinarily wouldn't have had a chance to make it to the NHL. Buzinski (also known as "Puckgoinski") was one of those players. Even under those circumstances, he didn't last long. After allowing 32 goals in just four games, he was shipped off to oblivion by the Rangers.

But not before Dan Daniel, the great New York sportswriter, had a chance to observe Puckgoinski's goaltending technique: "Steve showed a new technique," wrote Daniel. "He adopted the falling system. Persuaded that he who drops over the disk need not have fears of it being elsewhere, Buzinski spent more time on the ice than a mackerel in cold storage."

How to Talk Goalie

George Plimpton's wonderful book about hockey, *Open Net*, contains a character named "Seaweed" (actually Jim Pettie, then a goalie with the Boston Bruins) who uses lots of goalie slang. Here is a sampling of Pettie's cool-cat goalie lingo:

"Chirping"—the hockey equivalent to talking trash

"Candy-ass"—a wimp (not exclusive to hockey)

"Mucking it up"—popular term for getting physical on the ice, going into the corners after the puck

"Between the pipes" or "in the cell"—in goal

"In the shed"—Russian goalie expression for being in goal

"Being in the barrel"—old-fashioned term for being in the net

"The Big O"—standing ovation, what all players want

"Gassed"—cut from a team, what no players want

"Up on the roof"—a shot that comes in high towards a goalie

"Pumpkin," "coconut," "melon"—names for the head, where goalies get hit a lot

"He's got no seeds"—derogatory term for a player with no guts, i.e., balls

"Ringing the berries"—a shot that hits a player's cup.

Goalie Poet

Jim Pettie played backup on the Bruins to Gerry Cheevers, a Hall of Fame goalie. Cheevers had a lively wit too. Gump Worsley and

Andy Brown were the last goalies to wear a mask. Cheevers once described the NHL goaltending fraternity as "my twenty-six lodge brothers behind the masks and the two nuts without them." Cheevers never got into fights, because, he said, "I'm not sure I can lick my lips." He stuck fast to this rule, just as he did not engage in the traditional postgame handshakes. "I never shake hands after a game, because I don't believe in it," he said.

Cheevers maintained a certain perspective about hockey, even when things went bad. This may be a key to goalie survival; otherwise the pressure will overwhelm you. After the Bruins got demolished in a game, with Cheevers in goal, he composed this little ditty:

> "Roses are red
> Violets are blue
> They got ten
> We only got two."

Luckily for Cheevers there weren't many games like that, or even a keen sense of humor wouldn't have kept him afloat long in the NHL.

THE GIRAFFE

Ken Dryden, the great goaltender for the Canadiens—they've had a few of them, haven't they?—stood 6-4 with a wingspan to match. "He's got arms like a giraffe," said Phil Esposito. Do giraffes have arms? No matter. We get the message, Phil. Dryden's arms were long and gangly and they frustrated guys like Esposito, who were trying to slip a small black rubber thing past them. "Trying to jam one in on him is like trying to walk between two streetcars," said Johnny Bucyk, who, like Esposito, was a member of the Bruins and who, also like Espo, got frustrated trying to score off Dryden.

Dryden was one of the tallest and smartest goaltenders ever.

He attended law school at McGill University while playing for
the Canadiens and later became an attorney. "I was reading a
book of trusts and I fell asleep," he said, explaining why he was
late to a team meeting one morning. "There's nothing like trusts
to put you to sleep." His teammates on the Canadiens looked at
him as if he had just arrived from another planet.

Dryden was very intense on the ice. He never thought twice
about ragging on a teammate if he was not playing up to the level
that the man in goal demanded. Dryden was like a coach on the
ice and smarter than most coaches on the bench. He made a
speech a few years ago about what it was like to play for Montreal. The speech says as much about the Montreal organization
as it does about the high level of intelligence and skill that Dryden brought to hockey.

"In Montreal," said Dryden, "it never seemed to matter much
just who owned the team. What did matter was who wore the
sweaters and who scored the goals. That's why people paid their
money and went to games, and the Canadiens' owners never forget that. They may have enjoyed getting their names in the papers, being central to the main topic of conversation around the
city, but they never pretended to be more important to the success of the team than they were or ever could be. They let public attention focus on, they gave responsibility to, those who could
and had to deliver." In Montreal, Ken Dryden was one of those
who delivered.

SAMURAI BILLY WHIPS THE OILERS

In the early 1980s the most dominant team in hockey was the
New York Islanders. But riding out of the West came a team to
challenge them: Wayne Gretzky and the Edmonton Oilers. The
Oilers were young and brash and that irritated the hell out of the
champion Islanders. "We want to beat them more than anything.
You know why?" said Clark Gillies, a winger on the Islanders.

"Because they think they're the greatest thing since sliced bread." Added Bob Bourne, also of the Isles: "They think they're so hot. The thing that really bugs us is they don't give us any respect. The Flyers respect us. The Bruins respect us. The Rangers respect us. Edmonton doesn't respect us."

Well, the Oilers were pretty good all right, even if they didn't show the proper respect for their elders. But the Islanders were pretty good too—check that: in their prime, they were great—and they had a goalie named Billy Smith, who didn't take guff from nobody, as the saying goes. Oiler right-winger Glenn Anderson skated into Smith territory during the 1983 Cup finals and nearly got his head taken off with a deftly placed stick. "Anderson was viciously attacked," fumed Oiler coach Glen Sather. "Smith deliberately clubbed him. He swings his goal stick like a hatchet. Hopefully somebody on our team will take care of the problem."

Asked about Sather's charge, Smith did not back down. "If they run me and hurt me, or anybody else on our team, then we have to get even." Smith even launched a smoke bomb in the direction of Edmonton's most-protected asset: "Then it may be Gretzky," he warned.

Making threats at Edmonton's No. 1 citizen was tantamount to invading the city with tanks. The citizenry rose up in arms. The *Edmonton Journal* ran a full-page photograph of Smith with the headline *Public Enemy One*. The *Journal*—not exactly a model of journalistic objectivity at this moment—referred to Smith as "Mr. Obnoxious" and "Samurai Billy," saying that his sticking it to Anderson was "the latest in a hockey career that reads like a dossier on Jack the Ripper." The paper even ran an article quoting a hotel security guard who allegedly saw Smith snub a young autograph-seeker. "That guy is a real creep," the guard told a *Journal* reporter. "I saw a three-year-old kid come up for an autograph and Smith just brushed him off."

Smith got the last laugh, however. He brushed off Gretzky

and the Oilers and the Islanders won that emotional 1983 series, taking their fourth consecutive Stanley Cup in the
process.

A WAY-COOL GOALIE

Wayne Gretzky considered Grant Fuhr one of the greatest goalies
ever. The fact that the two played together on those great Edmonton Oiler teams of the 1980s may have had something to do
with Gretzky's opinion. Still, Fuhr was a very fine goalie who
maintained the level of cool you need to succeed in the net in the
NHL. After a game in the 1987 Stanley Cup finals, Fuhr went off
and played a couple of rounds of golf as a way to relax. A reporter
was aghast. "How could you play 36 holes of golf in the middle
of the Stanley Cup finals?" he asked. Said Fuhr: "Because there
wasn't time to play 54."

SHORT STUFF

San Jose Sharks goalie Arturs Irbe is as big as a minnow, but he
is hardly shark bait when it comes to standing up to the big guys.
He collided with Detroit's Keith Primeau—all 6-4, 220 pounds
of him—and knocked Primeau every which way but loose. Tie
Domi skated up to Irbe and said he was going to mash him. "You
should do that," said Irbe, not backing down. "You should try to
do *something* interesting."

"Interesting" would be one way to describe Irbe's stickhandling, which is not one of his better qualities. "I've often said Arturs should get paid more, because he makes the game so much
more exciting," said Sharks coach Kevin Constantine, referring
to those scary times when Irbe ventures away from the net. Others are more blunt. "Irbe is handling the puck badly," said one
writer, "or is that redundant?" Still, Irbe is an appealing charac-

Gump Worsley played in the days before masks and ridiculed any
goalies who wore them. "Anybody who wears a mask is scared," he said.
Photo by Bruce Bennett

ter. As Scott Ostler says, "How can you not like a pro athlete who
lists one of his hobbies as miniature golf? Although at his size,
what other kind of golf could Irbe play?"

OTHER GOALIES WE HAVE KNOWN

Look up *baby-faced* in *Webster's* and you will see a picture of Red
Wings goaltender Chris Osgood. "He doesn't look like the pa-
perboy," said Detroit GM Bryan Murray. "He looks like the pa-
perboy's little brother." Another Osgood description by Lowell
Cohn: "Instead of looking like a goalie who stops pucks flying at
him at warp speed, he seems as if he should be working as a bag-
ger in the supermarket, wearing a bow tie and saying, 'Paper or
plastic?'"

Sad is the story of old-time Blackhawk goalie Charlie Gardiner, who died shortly after his team won the Stanley Cup. "I think his whole life was shortened by goaltending," said teammate Johnny Gottselig. "He was always alone. Goalies are probably the loneliest guys in the world." . . . Ed Van Impe must've also been a lonely guy. Van Impe was a defenseman on those Stanley Cup–winning Flyer teams in the 1970s. Asked what made Van Impe such a good defenseman, his teammate goalie Bernie Parent responded, "He farts a lot."

Goalies storing water bottles on top of their net is now a common practice. But when Philadelphia goalie Pelle Lindbergh did it in the 1985 Stanley Cup finals, Edmonton Oiler coach Glen Sather had a fit. "Maybe we want a bucket of chicken on our net," said Sather. "Or a bucket of chicken on their net. Maybe hamburgers. I mean, if you have a water bottle out there, let's have lunch." All right, Glen. You bring the wine, we'll bring the cheese and bread.

Vancouver's Cliff Ronning caused a mini-controversy during the 1994 Cup finals when he criticized Ranger goalie Mike Richter. "We knew we could get to Richter, because his angles are so poor," said Ronning. Richter played the angles well enough to lead New York to its first Stanley Cup win in half a century. . . . The sterling play of Patrick Roy during the Canadiens' 1994 playoff series against Boston made news in the United States, where a national debate over health care was taking place. Cracked comedian Stu Silverstein: "Canadiens goalie Patrick Roy, after being admitted to a Canadian hospital for acute appendicitis, was given a fistful of antibiotics without surgery and sent out to play against the Bruins. So much for the Canadian health care system."

In April 1994, twenty-one-year-old Manon Rheaume played her first game as goalie of the Atlanta Knights of the International Hockey League, the first woman ever to play professional hockey. The pioneering Rheaume turned down *Playboy*'s $50,000 offer to pose nude and has even learned to handle male chauvinist sportswriters. After the historic game a sportswriter asked, "Did you break a nail?" and Manon managed a smile in reply.

PROFILES IN GOALIE COURAGE

Asked why he always shaved before a game, goalie Lorne Chabot said, "I stitch better when my skin is smooth." Chabot played in the era before masks, but goalies are still among the bravest of athletes. Beginning with Chabot himself, some profiles in goaltender courage:

"Chabot jumped into the air to stop a backhanded shot from the stick of Nels Stewart. Chabot misjudged it, and the puck caught him over the left eye. He fell in a heap to the ice, writhing in agony."
> —Montreal reporter, witnessing an injury to goalie Lorne Chabot

"One shot he stopped with his head in a tumultuous third period. Blood poured from a gash under his eye. Mowers refused to delay the game to be sewed up. He tended goal the last five minutes with blood streaming down his face."
> —Newspaper account of Detroit goalie Johnny Mowers's refusal to leave a 1943 Stanley Cup game

"His nose was broken 7 times, he picked up 175 stitches in his face, and once he almost lost an ear lobe when it was sliced by a careening puck."
> —Columnist Trent Frayne, on goalie Eddie Johnston's injury-filled career, typical for a goalie

"They kept taking me to the operating room in case a blood clot at the back of my head moved and they had to drill a hole. My weight went from 194 to 155 in the first week."
> —Eddie Johnston of the Bruins, after being knocked unconscious by a Bobby Orr slap shot in practice

Best Goalie Bumpersticker

"Only God Saves More Than Parent."
> —Spotted on a Philadelphia car, when Bernie Parent was holding forth in goal for the Flyers

Best Analysis of One Goalie's Weakness

"If Mikhail has a weakness, it's between his legs."
> —Broadcaster Brian Hayward, after Anaheim goalie Mikhail Shtalenkov allowed a goal

8

COACHES: THE MEN BEHIND THE BENCH

t's interesting to note where coaches stand in the NHL during games and compare it to the old Soviet system. In the
former Soviet Union, in its heyday one of the world's foremost hockey powers, the coach stood in front of his players—
a sign, if one was needed, of his supreme power—assuming he
won. If he didn't, he'd be on the first train to Siberia. In the NHL,
by contrast, the coach stands behind his players sitting on the
bench. With their high salaries and celebrity profiles, the players
come first in the pros. Until, that is, they start losing. Then they
all get out of the way for the coach, who, inevitably, is the poor
sap who loses his job first.

COACHING MAXIMS

"Every coach is an interim coach."
> —Ron Smith, former interim Rangers
> coach

"You yell at them today, they laugh at you, and then you're gone."

> —Jenny Roberts, hockey coach, on the difficulty in disciplining the modern player

"Who gets fired? The players? You know who's going to get the ax, don't you? It'll be the coach. How many goals does a coach let in? But he's the one to go."

> —Hal Laycoe, issuing the coach's lament, prior to being fired by Vancouver

"Coaching is like being a king. It prepares you for nothing."
> —Herb Brooks, former Olympic and NHL coach

"Any coach who believes he's deciding the game is fooling himself."

> —Mike Sertich, college hockey coach

"Be sure you finish first."

> —Rudy Pilous, after being fired as coach of the Blackhawks, asked if he had any advice for his successor

"I'll take a young pair of legs over an old head anytime."

> —Dick Irvin, ex-coach and Hall of Fame player

"Being behind the bench is the best job in hockey."
> —Punch Imlach

EVERY COACH'S PREDICAMENT

Every coach knows his time is limited, that he was hired to be fired. Even the greatest know that. Punch Imlach was one of the greatest. He coached Toronto to four Stanley Cup titles in the

1960s. Still, even his job wasn't secure—rather, it was as secure as any coach's, which means that it was like standing in quicksand. During his years with the Leafs, Punch received a telegram from the board of directors of the Maple Leaf Gardens, and it perfectly sums up every coach's predicament:

"PUNCH," said the telegram, "WE'RE WITH YOU ALL THE WAY—WIN OR TIE."

THEY DON'T LIKE MIKE

Mike Keenan shows how fast a coach can fall, in the public's esteem if nowhere else. In June 1994 he was on top of the world, having coached the New York Rangers to their first Stanley Cup title since the invention of the hockey stick. Why, Mike was so happy he even smiled. "When Rangers Captain Mark Messier carried the Cup to the bench," commented one sportswriter on the frenetic Madison Square Garden celebration, "Keenan came completely unglued and actually smiled."

Keenan is known for his dour demeanor and taskmaster ways. His nickname in Chicago was "Dolf," as in Adolf Hitler. He holds the men he is coaching in such disregard that "his ultimate dream would be to win the Stanley Cup without players," a former player of his has said. Steve Thomas recalled what it was like to play under Keenan in Chicago: "You might have a bad shift, and he would be all over you. And then he'd send you out again, and you might have another bad shift, and he'd be all over you again. He would just grate on you and finally you'd snap," said Thomas, adding, "Eventually he just drove us physically and mentally insane." An NHL executive sums up the Keenan style more succinctly: "The problem with Keenan is he's a Marine drill sergeant, but there is no graduation date."

But Keenan gets results, and that's why his players put up with him. But now he's known for something else, and it's nothing to smile about. Exercising a loophole in his contract, Keenan ditched the Rangers and jumped to the St. Louis Blues, who gave him a ton of money and more control. New York fans were up in arms. The city's tabloids branded Keenan a traitor, claiming that he lied about published reports during the playoffs that he was in secret negotiations with the Detroit Red Wings about taking over as coach there. Keenan said there were no such negotiations and that he would remain as coach of the Rangers. A month after winning the Cup, he had quit the Rangers and was talking again with the Red Wings and the Blues, the team that eventually landed him.

Needless to say, Iron Mike's actions left an unpleasant taste in the Big Apple. *Sports Illustrated* described Keenan as a man with "an arena-sized ego" and "a power-hungry egotist who has gone out on a sour note wherever he has been." And, referring to coaches in every sport in both the colleges and pros who demand team play from their players while going for the best deal for themselves, the magazine concluded, "Perhaps Keenan is in the right place at last. But the Blues should take note: For a man who demands team play of his charges, Keenan has proved to be any-thing but a team player himself."

THE WORLD ACCORDING TO FRED

One of the winning-est coaches of all time, Fred Shero steered the often bumpy course for the famous (infamous?) Broad Street Bullies, the Stanley Cup–winning Philadelphia Flyer teams of the 1970s. In addition to his coaching abilities, Shero had a lively wit and a gift for aphorisms. Some of the things Shero has said are some of the most memorable things anybody has ever said about the game of hockey. Some samples:

On coping with pressure: "The only people not under stress are dead."

On how he views people: "People can be divided into three types: those who make things happen, those who watch things happen, and those who wonder what happened. In which category are you?"

On a scouting trip he took to the distant regions of Canada: "It was so far north that if you opened your car window you'd be shaking hands with Santa Claus."

After hearing that some of the younger players on the team didn't like Shero's edict against long hair and mustaches: "It will take time for them to conform. But they will conform. If they don't—well, Jean Beliveau retired and Gordie Howe retired and we still have hockey."

On the game of hockey: "Hockey is a children's game played by men. Since it is a children's game, the men who play it should have fun."

On the importance of hustle: "There are no heroic tales without heroic tails."

On fighting and talking in hockey: "Fighting and talking are both part of the game. Hockey is just a love affair when you don't have fighting. As for talking, you show me a team you can talk to, and I'll show you a team you can beat."

On his goal-scoring philosophy: "I don't like to score too quickly on the power play. I'd rather run 'em around for two minutes."

Assessing a 7-6 win by the Flyers over Montreal: "Montreal played one goal dumber than us."

On why he was visiting Russia after his team had won the Stanley Cup: "I've already taught them everything I know. The only way they're going to get better is if I get smarter."

On success and failure: "Success requires no explanation. Failure presents no alibis."

On his loyalty to his players: "There are things I would do for my players that I wouldn't do for my sons."

On charges that his Philadelphia clubs played too rough: "If you keep the opposition on their butts, they don't score goals. If you want to see pretty skating, go to the Ice Capades."

DISCIPLINING PLAYERS TODAY: ONE COACH'S OPINION

Are hockey players harder to handle today than they used to be? Milt Schmidt, former Boston Bruin coach and GM, says yes. Says Schmidt:

"I think that in my day asking for discipline was much easier than it is now. The salaries weren't all that great and there was always somebody looking over your shoulder trying to get your job. Today you've got so many teams, a player can tell a team that if they don't want him he'll go across the street and play for someone else. I admire any coach who can get it out of present players."

WHAT COACHES LOOK FOR IN PLAYERS

"I want size, and I want meanness."
> —Ed Snider (actually a Flyer executive)

"If they can fit through the door, I don't want 'em."
> —Milt Schmidt, former coach of the Bruins

SCOTTY'S DISASTER

Scotty Bowman is one of the greatest coaches in NHL history, but the 1994 Stanley Cup playoffs did not treat him very kindly. His Detroit Red Wings lost to the San Jose Sharks in seven games, and Bowman and the Wings took a pounding. "If Scotty is so brilliant," observed San Francisco sportswriter Lowell Cohn, "then who's that guy running back and forth behind the Detroit bench screaming at his players and acting as if he doesn't have a clue?" Earlier, Cohn described the winningest coach in NHL history this way: "He's a small, stocky guy who was wearing a black trench coat. Any second, you expected him to open it up, reveal-

ing fifty watches dangling from the lining, at which point he'd offer to sell you a Rolex dirt cheap."

The Detroit press, as is its way, was even nastier. Keith Gave
of the *Free Press* said that Bowman was outcoached by Kevin
Constantine of the Sharks. The Wings, said Gave, were "lulled
into playing San Jose's game—no-hit hockey," and it was Bowman's fault. "Bowman seems to be so worried about taking penalties that he has taken his own toughest players out of the game,"
wrote Gave, who was not in a giving mood. *Detroit News* columnist Bob Wojnowski was also critical of the Wings' lackadaisical
play: "If you went to bed early Tuesday night, you might have
missed the Red Wings doing the same. Fluff up a pillow and turn
down the lights. The Wings are getting that sleepy look, like
they're ready for another long off-season."

Sure enough, the Red Wings were. "We learned a lot Tuesday
night," continued Wojnowski. "We learned the Wings are like the

Scotty Bowman. "Complex, confusing, misunderstood, unclear in every
way but one. He is a brilliant coach, the best of his time."—*Ken Dryden*.
Photo courtesy of the Detroit Red Wings

bogus bully in the schoolyard, the one who keeps drawing lines in the dirt. Every time someone steps across the line, the Wings say they're really mad now and then draw another. One more line to cross and the Sharks will have a stunning Stanley Cup playoff win. One more line and the Wings will have an unfathomable collapse and face unthinkable scorn."

So that was the way it went for the Red Wings. Not only did they get beaten by the formerly toothless Sharks, their coach had a terrible time with doors during the series. Before a game Bowman retreated into a storage room at the San Jose Arena to collect his thoughts before facing the media. The door locked behind him, and Scotty had to pound on it until a worker heard the noise. But the keys weren't available, and while the worker went to look for them, word got around that Bowman was trapped in the room. "Keep him in there," laughed one of the Red Wing players.

The very next day, the Red Wings were practicing at another rink in San Jose, when there was a loud pounding at a side door. Everybody thought it was just some unruly fan trying to get inside, and nobody bothered to get it. "That's probably Scotty Bowman," joked a reporter. Finally, when the banging didn't stop, someone opened the door. It *was* Bowman.

KEEPING A LOW PROFILE

During that playoff series with Detroit, a reporter asked Sharks coach Kevin Constantine what he thought about the contention that he was outcoaching one of the masters of the craft, Scotty Bowman. Constantine is an intense young man whose face, said one columnist, "looks like a fist with red hair around the knuckles." But Constantine has already learned that being a successful coach means being a successful diplomat too.

"Do you want to know what I think on or off the record?" he told the reporter. "On the record, no comment."

Okay then, said the reporter, what about off the record?

"Off the record?" said Constantine. "It doesn't matter." Oh.

MORE THOUGHTS ON SCOTTY BOWMAN

"Abrupt, straightforward, without flair or charm, he seems cold and abrasive, sometimes obnoxious and controversial, but never colorful . . . He is complex, confusing, misunderstood, unclear in every way but one. He is a brilliant coach, the best of his time."

—Ken Dryden, who played for Bowman
on the Canadiens

"I feel sorry for Scotty. It must be tough dealing with twenty-four All-Stars."

—Fred Shero, on Bowman when he
coached the talented, though temperamental, Canadiens

"If I had been perfect I don't think he would have been satisfied. He was constantly badgering me from behind the bench. If nothing happened during the game that he could yap about, he'd start hollering about an earlier game, even if he hadn't been involved in it. When he questioned me it was always in a sneering, sarcastic way, as if he was trying to convince me I was inferior."

—Bruce Hood, former NHL referee

"When you coach against Scotty, you're the enemy. There are no friends. He was always one of those guys who was looking for an edge somehow, and he didn't care whether it offended you—that was the game he had to win tonight."

—Harry Neale, ex-NHL coach

OTHER COACHES WE HAVE KNOWN

John Brophy was so mad at his team for the way it was playing, he shut off the lights in the dressing room between periods. "You're playing like you're in the dark," he told his players, "so you might as well spend the intermission in the dark too.". . . Bill LaForge explained his credentials as a hockey coach this way: "If you're wondering about my credentials, I have my Ph.D. That's for pride, hustle, and desire.". . . Wren Blair, who coached Minnesota in the early days of expansion, was a hard guy to impress. When one of his players was bragging about scoring 50 goals in a season, Wren scoffed and said, "It's the ones after 50 that count."

The reason Red Wing coach Tommy Ivan worked his players so hard was so simple: "If you get them up early enough, they'll get to bed early enough.". . . Detroit's most glorious era was the 1949–55 period, when the Red Wings won four Stanley Cups and finished first seven straight times, an achievement rivaled only by the baseball Yankees. But Red Wing coach Jack Adams harrumphed when the Red Wings were called "the Yankees of hockey." Adams growled, "We are not the Yankees of hockey. The Yankees are the Red Wings of baseball." That's telling 'em, Jack!

"Dirty Bertie" Olmstead was coach and general manager of the old California Seals, an expansion team whose owner was Charlie O. Finley. The only man the players hated more than Olmstead was Finley. . . . "If I was a player I don't even know if I'd want to be associated with this bunch," Olmstead said about his team. "I'd be tossing a few of them out of that dressing room on their cans. They have no pride. A lot of them are getting a chance of a lifetime, and they act like playing in the NHL is a prison sentence." Playing for Olmstead on that Seals team *was* a prison sentence. As a former player of his said, "If Olmstead did public relations for Santa Claus, there wouldn't be any Christmas."

Phillipe "Phil" Watson of the New York Rangers was a native French speaker who had his problems with English. Trying to insult an older, washed-up player, Watson sputtered, "You're nothing but a been-has!" . . . After being introduced to Dallas coach Bob Gainey, reporter Randy Galloway said, "Bob, I don't know that much about the NHL, but give me two weeks and I'll be an expert." Gainey responded, "I've met your type before, but usually it's an owner.". . .

When Pat Burns accepted Coach of the Year honors in 1989, he uttered a sentiment that rang true for a lot of coaches: "I never wanted to be coach of the year. I just wanted to be coach for a year."... A team psychologist for Toronto says about Burns: "He can be an awful bastard sometimes." That probably rings true about a lot of coaches besides Burns. Whatever you think about the only ex-policeman currently coaching in the NHL, he's got a hairstyle that can't be topped. Lowell Cohn describes it as "a pompadour the size of a triple-decker club sandwich."

When he was hired to be coach of the Canadiens, Jacques De-mers told a radio interviewer, "I've got a three-year contract, which means I'll be coaching the Montreal Canadiens the next three years." Serge Savard, the former defenseman-turned-executive with Montreal, was sitting in on the interview. After hearing De-mers's statement, he interjected, "No, Jacques. That just means we have to pay you for the next three years." Serge had it right.

Three Coaches, Three Anecdotes

Here are three anecdotes about three of the greatest hockey men of all time: Toe Blake, Dick Irvin, and Lester Patrick.

1

Toe Blake, said the writer Red Fisher, was "a kindly old coach, a gentleman, and a son of a bitch, all in the same sentence." Blake was a coach, gentleman, and SOB for one of the greatest sporting dynasties of all time, the Montreal Canadiens, piloting the Habs to five straight Stanley Cup titles from 1956 to 1960. As one would expect from one of the winning-est coaches, Blake hated to lose. And he lost so seldom that he never learned how to do it very well. The third part of his personality—the SOB part—came out when his team lost. On one West Coast road trip the Canadiens had got-ten beaten up pretty bad, and on the way home their flight en-countered bad weather over the Rockies. The plane tossed and rocked and heaved, shaking up the crew and passengers.

Afterwards a relieved reporter who was on the flight said to Toe, "Rocky flight, eh?"

Still thinking about his team's losing streak, the surly Blake responded, "I wish the damn thing had crashed."

2

The early history of the New York Rangers is the story of New York hockey pioneer Lester Patrick. He coached the Rangers to two early Stanley Cup titles, before the Curse went into effect and the team fell on fifty years or so of hard times. "He struck dramatic poses and was in turn kind, sarcastic, pompous, vain, callous, and contrite, depending on the circumstances," said Frank Boucher, who played for Patrick on the Rangers. "He had both a compelling arrogance and a winning humility."

Patrick also acted as general manager for the Rangers for many years. He was tight as Scrooge with a penny, and it didn't matter if you were related to him or not. One of his best players was his son Lynn, who later became a Ranger coach himself. In his rookie season Lynn had made first-team NHL and scored a ton of goals for the Rangers on the left wing. So he asked his father for a raise. "I had a good year," he said.

"Yeah," said his father. "But I made sure you had good linemates."

3

It is as tough for a coach as it is for an athlete to know when to walk away. Dick Irvin was one of the rare ones who did it with grace. In his twenty-six-year coaching career in the NHL, he led Montreal to three Stanley Cup titles in the forties and fifties. In 1956, while coaching Chicago, he developed cancer and had to call it quits. Here is what he said to his Blackhawk players:

"Fellows, you know I've always told you that if you didn't give 100 percent you couldn't play on this team. Well, now I can't give you 100 percent, so I'm leaving. I can't coach anymore. I have to go home. Good luck."

And with that, he walked off.

HE'D FIRE HIS OWN BROTHER

Probably the least appealing of all of Glen Sather's accomplishments as a coach is that he saved Peter Pocklington's skin. After
Pocklington sold Wayne Gretzky to the highest bidder in 1988,
Oiler fans were ready to tar and feather the Edmonton owner.
Their boys had won two Stanley Cups in a row, and in dealing
their star player away, Pocklington clearly had other things on his
mind than going for a three-peat. But "Slats," as he is known,
steadied the helm and guided the Gretzky-less Oilers to yet another Stanley Cup in the 1989–90 season. Edmonton fans will
never forgive Pocklington for the Trade, but at least they could
accept.

That's not to say that relations between Sather and his players
were always harmonious. After the Oilers lost to Calgary in the
1986 playoffs, Sather jumped all over Gretzky for what he saw as
a lackluster performance. The Great One did not take kindly to
this criticism. "Slats was always a lousy loser, so rather than accept the loss, he bought out of it altogether," said Gretzky later.
"All of a sudden, for the first time in a long time we were down,
and what did Slats do? He kicked us."

Mostly, though, those Oilers did the kicking. They were a marvelous band, and in many people's minds, they rescued the game
from the clutches of the Philadelphia Flyers and other teams that
played the bully-boy style of hockey. They included Gretzky and
Mark Messier and Paul Coffey—one reporter compared him to
"a bird in flight" when he was skating—and many more. After the
offensive-minded Oilers won the 1984 Cup, their first ever,
sportswriter Jack Falla had a great line: "The sleek," he said, "shall
inherit the ice." And so they did, at least for the decade.

The man in charge was the small, yet pugnacious, Sather.
When he played in the NHL, he and teammate Bryan Watson
were described as "relatively small rogues" by writer Gary Ronberg. Ronberg added that the two men "do not intimidate play-

ers, but they have a knack of unnerving them with an imperti-
nent word or gesture, an annoying slash or check."

Both Watson and Sather were intense competitors even as
Bryan became coach of the Oilers and Glen became GM. But
when Edmonton was not performing up to expectations, Sather
did not hesitate to fire his good friend and appoint himself coach.
Asked how he could let such a longtime friend go, Sather replied,
"If my own brother was coaching this club, or playing on it, and
it wasn't working out, I'd let him go too."

KEEPING HIS PRIORITIES STRAIGHT

Tom McVie once coached the New Jersey Devils and, in a classic line, expressed the frustration that all coaches—hockey or otherwise—encounter when dealing with their sometimes reluctant
charges. "I have four guys who don't understand a word I'm saying, ten guys who do understand but don't do a thing I tell them
to do, and another four who aren't good enough to do what I tell
them to do," said McVie. Nevertheless, McVie had a long and
fruitful career as an NHL coach in part because he had his priorities straight. "You love hockey more than you love me," his
wife said to him one night.

"Yes," replied Tom, "but I love you more than I love baseball."

9

BEFORE THEY WORE HELMETS: STARS OF YESTERDAY

Was the old-time game better than hockey today? Naw, not even close. But one thing was better in the old days, at least from the fan's point of view. The players didn't all wear helmets, so you could really see what they looked like. "If I had my way," an NHL owner said some years ago, "I'd toss every helmet in the trash can. I want my fans to see each of my players as a different personality." For better or worse, though, those days are probably gone for good, and helmeted hockey players are here to stay.

REMEMBERING DEREK (AND THE THINGS HE SAID)

Derek Sanderson was to hockey what Joe Namath and Muhammad Ali were to football and boxing, respectively. "Outspoken, cocky, flippant"—these were the words they used to describe Derek. He wore beads, bell bottoms, and long hair in the styles of the times—the sixties and seventies—and women loved him just like they did Broadway Joe. Also, Derek could play some hockey. Even on a Boston Bruin team with the likes of Bobby Orr

"If you're going to win the Stanley Cup," said the flashy Derek Sanderson, "you've got to go top shelf." And he certainly did. Photo by Bruce Bennett

and Phil Esposito, Derek stood out, as much for his abilities on the ice as the things he said and did off it.

Sanderson is a hockey broadcaster now, but it's still fun to turn back the time machine and plug into his off-the-wall comments from those days. Clearly, a lot of what Derek said was designed to outrage and entertain, and he certainly did that. Some samples:

On the values of going to college: "All the formal education in the world isn't going to help you when you're standing at the left point."

On his high-living lifestyle: "If you're going to win the Stanley Cup, you've got to go top shelf."

On playing rough: "If I have to hit a guy and hurt him to win, I'll hit him and hurt him. If a guy is afraid of being hurt, I'll give him the stick all night long."

On how to win a hockey fight: "The trick in hockey fights is to throw the first punch. The guy who does that usually wins."

On how to win a faceoff: "One of the key elements to winning a faceoff is cheating. You've got to cheat, because it's too difficult to win most of them fair and square."

On his dining habits while travelling: "My pregame meal on the road is a steak and a blonde."

On youth hockey in Canada: "The sweepcheck is a great play, but not too many guys use it anymore, because hockey players are mass produced in Canada and most kids are no longer taught the subtleties of the game."

On famed junior coach Hap Emms: "The cheapest coach of all time . . . In Canada, Hap Emms was the god of junior hockey, which gives you some idea how a guy's image can run away from the real man. He fooled and befuddled everybody."

On his habit of shooting after the whistle blows: "Some goalies get rattled when I shoot after a whistle. So I'll take the shot. If it bothers them, that's fine. I'll do anything to win."

On the goaltenders for the St. Louis Blues, Glenn Hall and Jacques Plante: "There aren't many better goaltenders in hockey than Hall. He's a class guy, which is more than I can say for the Blues' other goalie, Jacques Plante, who is a prima donna and a wise guy. Plante once made a crack that Hall was the best backup goalie in hockey, which is like telling a Moslem that Allah is the best backup God in the world. The players don't like Plante."

After the Bruins won three straight games from the St. Louis Blues in the 1970 Stanley Cup finals: "We have tougher workouts in practice than we've had in our games with the Blues."

After downing two beers, he remarked on his drinking habits: "This isn't drinking. If I get into the rye, then I'm drinking."

DEREK WEARS WHITE SHOES (ALMOST)

Derek Sanderson was as flamboyant as they come. Once he even considered wearing white skates, the way his idol Joe Namath styled around in white cleats on a football field. Sanderson thought about it long and hard until Harry Sinden, the Bruins GM, weighed in on the subject. "If the guy wants to order white skates," Sinden barked, "order him a pink helmet to go with them." Sanderson decided not.

SANDERSON: FIGHTER OR PHONY?

For all of Sanderson's tough-guy rhetoric, some players around the NHL thought he was a phony—that he *should* have worn that pink helmet. "The guy isn't a fighter," said Cliff Koroll, then with the Blackhawks. "He's always starting things when he has an advantage, and then he disappears in the crowd when the going gets rough. He's good at the cop-out."

Brad Park, the great defenseman for the New York Rangers, had the same criticism. "Sanderson talks a lot about his fighting ability and his willingness to mix," said Park. "The facts are a bit different. When he does fight he throws two or three punches and then backs off because he knows he can't handle most guys after that."

Park considered Sanderson an overrated blowhard, and never missed an opportunity to bash him, at least verbally. "I got to my hotel room and turned on the television and there was Derek Sanderson, Mr. Wise Guy of the Bruins," Park wrote in his book. "As usual his comments made me sick." Sanderson just got on Park's nerves. The reason? "He opens his mouth when he shouldn't," said Park. "Like a small boat in distress, he ought to shape up." Nor did Park like Sanderson's on-ice style either. "What bothers me most about Sanderson is his flakiness; at any given time he doesn't know what he's going to do and he has no concept of hockey ethics."

No concept of hockey ethics? By a man who always got in the first punch, cheated at faceoffs, and shot the puck after the whistle blew? Even Sanderson himself might agree with Park on that one.

BRAD PARK, ON THE BRUINS

Brad Park didn't just have it in for Sanderson; he didn't like any of those Big, Bad Bruins, as they were called. "Bloodthirsty animals," is what he called them at one point. "The Bruins," said Park, commenting on Boston's roughhouse hockey style, "have turned present-day hockey into a brutal sport." That is what he had to say in general; here is what he had to say about the Bruins, in specific.

On Phil Esposito: "He's an extraordinary stickhandler and a superb shooter, but he doesn't have any guts. He's carried by the animals on the Boston team."

More from Park on Esposito: "A lot of people don't realize it, but Esposito gets annoyed—more than the average player—when he's taken out of a play."

On one of Boston's top scrappers, Johnny McKenzie: "His bag is running at people from behind. No player really objects to getting hit straight on, but when a guy rams you from behind that's bad news. McKenzie symbolizes the bush style of the Boston hockey club."

On Boston's enforcer, Ted Green, receiving a fractured skull in the infamous 1969 stick fight with Wayne Maki: "Many people believe Green got exactly what he deserved, because he was nothing more than a hatchet man. After he recovered and returned to the NHL, I thought he might have learned something from the experience. But he hasn't. He's still carrying his stick high and doing the same dumb things he did before he was hurt."

Again, Park on Ted Green: "It's people like Green who give hockey a bad name. He can't be trusted. He swings at players with his stick, and his stick is always up."

SNIPING AT BOBBY

Brad Park even had unkind words to say about the great Bobby Orr, one of the best of all time. Said Park: "One of the myths about hockey is that Bobby Orr is unstoppable . . . Another myth about Orr is that he's a gentlemanly and clean player. Actually, Orr can be a hatchetman just like some of his Boston teammates." Furthermore, said Park, Orr's concept of hockey ethics resembled that of teammate Derek Sanderson. "Another thing about Orr is that he doesn't like to get hit, and sometimes he'll throw a cheap shot at one of our guys. A man of his ability needn't revert to such stuff, but he does."

Now, some of Park's criticisms can be attributed to his fiercely competitive nature, and Bruin fans may point out that Park's hostility may be due to the fact that Orr, Esposito, Sanderson et al. mostly kicked his Ranger teams up and down the ice. But other people besides Park have criticized Orr. Former NHL referee Bruce Hood said that Orr was "one of the must difficult players" he ever came up against. "He had as foul a mouth as any player I ever came across," said Hood. "Some nights he'd stand ten feet away from me and call me a 'fucking idiot,' or unleash a torrent of abuse."

Stan Fischler, the journalist, also had troubles with Orr. "Bobby Orr hides from reporters and, when caught, answers questions evasively, with little frankness," said Fischler. Evading reporters hardly constitutes a capital offense, but Fischler thought Orr was overrated as well. "As a defenseman he is not all that good defensively," Fischler maintained, arguing that late in his career Orr was highly overrated. "The case for Bobby Orr as the world's best hockey player has been made so many times it has become as much of a bromide as declaring 'Britannia Rules the Waves,'" wrote Fischler, who thought that Orr was indeed a "superb" hockey player, just not "the best."

We'll leave such fine distinctions to others, far preferring the sentiments of Canadien great John Ferguson— "He was in a class above the superstars," said Fergy about Orr—or one of Orr's teammates on the Bruins, Don Awrey. "I played in the Orr era," said Awrey. "These other defenseman, like Denis Potvin, Brad Park, Larry Robinson, Serge Savard, Borje Salming, good as they were, they couldn't carry his skates."

Two More Thoughts on Bobby

"He could thread a needle with a puck, shoot it like a bullet or float it soft. Orr was the only player who could dictate the tempo of the game, speed it up or slow it down. He could see the whole ice the way a spectator sees it from above."

> —Eddie Johnston, Orr's teammate on the Bruins

"Kid, I don't know what they're paying you, but it's not enough."

> —Bruins defenseman Ted Green to a young Bobby Orr, after Orr faked him out at a team scrimmage

The Family that Fights Together

Bobby Orr came from a strong family background. That was one of his strengths as a player and a person. Doug Orr, Bobby's father, once gave a piece of advice to Carl Lindros, Eric's father. The advice was simple: "Keep your kid a kid." That's not easy to do when your son is a budding young hockey superstar. There are endless distractions. People do things for you because you're perceived to be special, but they also pick on you for that same reason. So what do you do? Well, if you're a member of the Orr family, you stick together. One time Bobby got into the middle of a fight along the boards in juniors. He was outmatched physically and getting the worst of it when, all of a sudden, a woman started hitting Bobby's opponent over the head with her purse.

"You big brute," she yelled as she hit. "Leave Bobby alone!"

It was Bobby's sister.

The Master of the Slap Shot

Bobby Hull was, for a time, the Michael Jordan of hockey. While playing for the Chicago Blackhawks in the 1960s, he be-

Bobby Hull in his prime.
Goalie Les Binkley said
about Hull's famous slap
shot: "It starts off looking
like a small pea and then
disappears altogether."
Photo by Bruce Bennett

came the biggest name in hockey and the biggest thing in
Chicago sports. "I played fifteen years in Chicago and I owned
the city," he said once. "I owned the people." He wasn't exaggerating.

Hull could skate like a dream, but what most people remember about him was his shot. To make another sports comparison,
he was to hockey what Sandy Koufax and Nolan Ryan were to
baseball. He could "bring it"—shoot the puck—at unbelievable
speeds. "It starts off looking like a small pea and then disappears
altogether," said goalie Les Binkley about Hull's slap shot. This
million-mile-an-hour shot was every goalie's nightmare. "The
one that scares me the most is Bobby Hull," said Gerry Des-
jardins, another goalie of that time. "He scares every goalie. He's
built like a bull and skates like the wind and he shoots from everywhere. He uses one of those curved sticks and the puck whistles
in and curves and dances and sort of explodes on you. He can
drive you into the net with a shot."

But of all the goalies, Philadelphia's Bernie Parent seemed to know how to handle Hull the best. Asked what he did when Bobby pulled his stick back to shoot, Parent answered, "Try not to get hit."

BOBBY HULL'S PHYSIQUE

Bobby Hull, said one observer, "was an ice-bound Astaire." Yes, but he had a body like Hercules. If Hull hadn't been a hockey player, he might have gotten work as a freight train. Not driving a freight train or loading one—an actual freight train. Okay, so we exaggerate. But the Hull physique was the kind that spawned exaggeration. Here are two more accounts:

"He can still vividly recall going up to Bobby Hull's hotel room with a buddy to 'meet the Golden Jet.' Bobby Hull was lying on the bed with his arms behind his head, and Dad says it seemed as if Hull's chest stretched from one side of the bed to the other."
—Eric Lindros, recalling the time his father first met Bobby Hull

"He's big enough to chase bears with sticks."
—Rival player, on Hull

THE SHADOW KNOWS . . . BUT DOESN'T PLAY FAIR

The concept of "shadowing" essentially began with Bobby Hull. Opposing coaches found they couldn't stop him any other way, so they assigned a player (such as Claude Provost) to stay with Hull and give him trouble wherever he went on the ice. Easier said than done. Even with only one player to think about, many shadows had a hard time staying with Hull and had to resort to Rejean Houle's defensive techniques. "When Bobby gets past me," said Houle, "I've got to trip him. It's the only way I can stop him."

The Difference between Sanderson and Bobby Hull

Both Bobby Hull and Derek Sanderson were NHL stars who jumped to the rival World Hockey Association in the early 1970s. Hull went to Winnipeg in the WHA, Sanderson to Philadelphia. Both got a ton of money for switching leagues. How they handled all that money, however, was quite different. "All this money, man," said Sanderson after he signed. "It's just unreal. I can do whatever the hell I want now. I might just buy myself the whole city."

The first time the Winnipeg Jets visited Philadelphia, Bobby Hull spent the day of the game signing autographs for kids. Derek, meanwhile, was off trying to buy the city. "That's the difference between a player like Hull and a player like Sanderson," commented sportswriter Stan Hochman. "Hull spent his day trying to earn his big salary, while all Derek could do was try to figure out how to spend his."

Two Hockey Legends Discuss Violence in Hockey

"Gordie, wouldn't this game be much nicer without the animals?"

> —Bobby Hull to Gordie Howe, as the two stood along the boards and watched a nasty fight among some of their Red Wing and Blackhawk teammates

What Bobby Hull Thinks about the Modern Game

In the early 1970s, when Hull was still playing, he didn't think much of the type of players who were coming into pro hockey. "There's been an influx of guys who don't put out every night," he said at the time. "There's no incentive left. Or at least there doesn't seem to be anything driving the players anymore."

Now that he's retired and an elder statesman of hockey, Hull still doesn't think much of today's players, although for different reasons. Here is what he said recently:

"Where have all the Stan Mikitas, Yvan Cournoyers, Henri Richards, and Davey Keons gone? The league used to be full of them. They were the guys who used to entertain royally. Those 5-9, 170-pounders aren't around, except the odd one, like Theoren Fleury. All you see are these big kookaloos. That's why the game looks like it's played by robots. They all play the same way, other than a chosen few. They're all like trees."

He goes on, "We used to do things for a reason. Mikita, Bobby Orr, and Gordie Howe did things for a reason. Now they don't have a reason. When we had the puck, we didn't want to give it away. Now, they work their rear end off to get the puck, then they dump it in. That doesn't make sense."

WHAT A FEW OTHERS THINK ABOUT THE MODERN GAME

"Contemporary hockey is an obscenity compared to what it was meant to be and what it once was."
                                        —Stan Fischler, writer

"Under current conditions hockey can't be played. The once intricate, balanced game has disintegrated into a mass mugging on skates."
                                        —Ed Linn, author

"The game of hockey is simply not the game it was in my day. Shooting was more accurate then. Passing cleverer. Stickhandling was an art practiced not by just a few but by many."
                                        —Rocket Richard, Hall of Fame hockey
                                        player

130

SLAP SHOTS

STAN THE MAN

Stan Mikita was one of the first NHL players to wear a helmet. The reason? "I want to spend the summers cutting grass rather than pushing up daisies," he said. Mikita was a teammate of Bobby Hull's on the Blackhawks and a wizard at faceoffs. Nobody could get his stick down the way Mikita did. Mikita was just as fast with one-liners. Referee Bruce Hood described him as "a pain in the neck" for all the smart remarks he made to Hood and his brethren. "He always had something sarcastic to say and wouldn't think twice about belittling an official on or off the ice," said Hood. Mikita might yell at a ref, "What the hell's going on here, you trying to ruin the game? They didn't come here to see you," and the fans in Chicago Stadium would be all over the guy. Still, Mikita won the Lady Byng Memorial Trophy for sportsmanship twice.

Mikita and Hull played together in Chicago until Bobby jumped to Winnipeg in the WHA. Mikita said that every night before he went to bed he used to face west and bow in the direction of Winnipeg, because after Hull left Chicago, management tripled his salary. After Mikita retired, a reporter asked him what he liked best about playing in the NHL. "The paycheck," he said. The reporter then asked what he liked least about the NHL. "The size of the paycheck," Mikita answered. Okay, then, what has been the biggest change in the league since you left? Naturally, Mikita answered, "The size of the paychecks."

MR. EVERYTHING

Some years ago, when it seemed like just about everybody was playing the board game "Trivial Pursuit," there was an easy way to score whenever a hockey question came up. Just answer "Gordie Howe." It didn't seem to matter what the question was concerning hockey, the answer was "Gordie Howe." And even if the answer did not happen to be "Gordie Howe," nobody could fault you if you answered him. Because, for many many years, he was hockey's "Mr. Everything."

And, to a certain degree, still is. He was hockey's Methuselah; he kept playing and playing and playing, thirty-two seasons in all, with Detroit in the NHL and then Houston in the WHA. His career stretches across history, from the end of World War II to 1980. He won the NHL scoring title six times, and until a fellow named Gretzky came along, nobody in the league put the puck in the net more than Gordie Howe. Howe was, in fact, Gretzky's idol—and there can be no finer compliment than that.

Although his name still remains at the top, or near the top, of most playing records in the NHL, the record books can't do justice to Gordie Howe. No record book can tell you what it was like to go into the corners after the puck against Gordie Howe. If it happened, it would almost certainly be Howe, not you, who'd come out with the puck. Your stick would be carrying air and all you'd have to show for your effort was a bruise.

"Look at those shoulders, see how they slope from his neck," said Red Wing coach Jack Adams, admiring Howe's build. "He used to hang from a door frame when he was a kid, developing those shoulder muscles. He could have been a prizefighter." Instead he put those muscles to work muscling up against enemy defensemen.

Howe used his elbows the way Errol Flynn used a sword. Another nickname for Gordie: "Mr. Elbows." Leo Boivin, a Maple Leaf defenseman, played against him many times and had the bruises to show for it. Leo was not a large man and stood just about eye level with Howe's elbows. "Poor Leo," said his coach Joe Primeau, watching Boivin undress after a game with his body full of bruises. "When he goes into the corners for the puck he's just the right height for Howe's elbows." Ouch.

Howe, said Gerald Eskenazi, was the "league's unofficial greeter." But no welcome wagon was he. The first time Brad Park faced him in a game, the skilled Ranger defenseman surprised him with a hard check. Howe responded with a slice of his hockey stick, barely missing Park's eye. "I'm young," said Park afterwards. "I'll have time to get even." A lot of his opponents said the same thing, but with Gordie Howe, they almost never did.

ONE TOUGH HOMBRE

You don't last thirty-two seasons in professional hockey being a pansy. Gordie Howe sure wasn't one. He came back from a brain concussion in a 1950 game that might have destroyed a lesser player's career. Some said he became an even tougher player after this incident, because he didn't want to be hit hard like that again. But did he play dirty? A few people thought so:

> *"Howe is a great player, but the dirtiest who ever lived."*
> —Carl Brewer, who played against Howe

> *"Howe is the dirtiest player in the league. The first time I ever played against him he gave it to me in the back of the knee, then he smashed my ribs and speared me in the stomach and the arm."*
> —Derek Sanderson

> *"He was a dirty hockey player, not tough, mind you, but dirty— and he would take absolutely nothing from nobody."*
> —Rocket Richard, one of Howe's greatest rivals

> *"It's such a shame such a great hockey player as Howe has to use his stick the way he does. Sometimes he carries it like a spear."*
> —Emile Francis, who coached against Howe

"You're working a game and you see a player is down. You know that Howe did it. But how can you prove it?"

> —NHL referee Vern Buffey, on how hard it was to catch Howe when he hit somebody

A FEW WELL-CHOSEN WORDS

Gordie Howe, like John Wayne, was a man of few words. But when he spoke, people listened. Here are a few well-chosen words of Gordie's, on a few topics close to his heart:

On how to prepare for going out on the ice: "Each time you go out, take two seconds to see who's on the ice so you'll know where trouble might come from and where help will be coming from."

On charges that he was a rough player: "Hockey is a man's game."

On what never to do in a game: "Don't drop your stick first."

After a reporter observed that Howe scored a lot of his points from rebounds after setting up in front of the net, Gordie said: "You don't score much from behind."

LOOK BACK IN ANGER (1)

Like Bobby Hull, Gordie Howe had some hard feelings about the way he was treated in the NHL, salarywise. Neither man felt he made as much as he deserved, and that was why they both ended up in the WHA. "Do you know that in my scoring title years and my Stanley Cup years I couldn't live on my hockey salary?" Howe said. "I had to take a summer job. Here I was, the star of the world, and I watched my neighbor, a salesman, take his family and his boat every Friday night for the weekend to their cottage. There I was, supposedly star of everything, working a second job to stay alive." So after leaving the NHL in 1971, Gordie signed with the Houston Aeros of the WHA. He not only got a healthy chunk of

After a reporter observed that he scored a lot of points from rebounds after setting up in front of the net, Gordie Howe replied, "You don't score much from behind." Photo courtesy of the Detroit Red Wings

money for it, but he also achieved the singular distinction of playing with his own sons, Mark and Marty, on the same professional hockey team.

LOOK BACK IN ANGER (2)

While we're on the subject of the Howes being mad at the NHL, let's not forget Colleen, Gordie's wife, who got really PO'ed when her gifted hockey-playing sons couldn't sign with the league because they were too young. At the time, the NHL would not allow clubs to draft anyone under the age of twenty. "It's an asinine rule," said Colleen. "Say you had a son who played the piano. You put a lot of time and money into coaching him and sending him to top conservatories. Then, at nineteen, when he's ready for Carnegie Hall, they tell you he can't play there because he's not old enough. That's ridiculous." The WHA had no such prohibitions, and its Houston franchise drafted—and signed—Colleen's boys, Mark and Marty, in 1973. Not only that, their old man decided to come along for the ride too. The NHL subsequently rescinded the rule.

THE ROCKET

Maurice "Rocket" Richard was one of the greatest-ever hockey players and perhaps its greatest goal scorer. One sportswriter dubbed him "the Special Delivery Kid" for the way he played hockey: everything in a rush. Said Montreal coach Toe Blake: "He lives for only one thing in life—to score goals." Another Montreal coach, Dick Irvin, compared him to Babe Ruth in his impact on hockey and the team he played for, the Montreal Canadiens. A rival of Gordie Howe's, the Rocket played with single-minded intensity, and his temper sometimes flared out of control. But his pell-mell rushes d√n the ice inspired observers to poetic flights of fancy. A sampling:

"Maurice Richard was the most exciting athlete I have ever seen. So much has been written about him that for me to offer a flood of new praise would be roughly equivalent to a Ph.D. candidate announcing he is going to prove that Hamlet *is an interesting play."*
                                   —Star Weekly Magazine

"When he's worked up, his eyes gleam like headlights. Not a glow, but a piercing intensity. Goalies have said he's like a motorcar coming at you at night. It's terrifying."
                              —Frank Selke, former managing director of the Canadiens

"It's a strange sensation coming in on you with his eyes popping like headlights."
                                   —Don Simmons, goalie

"I see this guy skating at me with wild hair and eyes just out of the nuthouse. 'Who's that?' I asked after the game. 'That's Mau-

rice Richard,' the guy said. 'He's a pretty good hockey player.'
'Yes,' I said, 'he is.'"

—Montreal executive Kenny Reardon,
on the first time he saw the Rocket play

"Quackenbush hurled his black-shirted body at Richard, but it
was as if he were checking a phantom."

—Stan Fischler, describing Bill Quackenbush's futile attempt to check a Rocket
rush

"Richard made his way through the Ranger defense like a pin-
ball bouncing his way past the obstacles to the goal."

—More from Stan Fischler

"His nerves are as taut as trout lines. If he had to keep the ten-
sion bottled up within himself, he'd probably blow up. Luckily
hockey provides a release for the nervous tension that twists his
stomach into knots and threatens a nervous breakdown."

—Author Vince Lunny on Richard's high-
strung temperament

"He had only Jim Thomson between him and the goal. Thom-
son may have been an All-Star defenseman, but they all looked
alike in those circumstances. He went around Thomson like a hoop
around a barrel."

—Dink Carroll, sportswriter

"The impact Richard had on the Canadiens and on the rest of
the league seems to me beautifully summed up in one incident that
occurred in Toronto. It was the time that, soaring head over heels
as the result of an artful Maple Leaf check, Richard shattered the
'unbreakable' Herculite glass that had just been installed in Maple
Leaf Gardens around the top of the boards. Richard put the heel

of his skate through it, and there was something perfect about its being the Rocket, the epitome of recklessness, of untrammeled fire and fury and abandon on the ice, who did it."
— Peter Gzowski, writer

"Twenty years from now we will edge our rocker up next to some crony on the porch of an old folks' home and say, 'Do you remember when the Rocket won those two big overtime games at Olympia in '51?' The Rocket is made to watch and write about."
—Columnist Bob Murphy, after the Rocket-
led Canadiens beat the Detroit Red Wings
in the 1951 Stanley Cup playoffs

ANOTHER THING ABOUT THE ROCKET

Another thing to remember about the Rocket was that he was one hairy dude. "God, he looked like an ape," said an awestruck Bill Gadsby, upon seeing Richard without his shirt on. "He had more hair over his body than anyone I'd ever seen. There was hair actually sticking up in the air from his shoulders." A Montreal front-office man put it another way: "If he had another hair on his back, he'd be up a tree."

HOW WOULD ROCKET DO TODAY?

How would Rocket Richard fare if he was playing hockey today? Broadcasters Dick Irvin and Harry Neale were mulling this over on the air a few seasons back. Dick asked Harry how many goals he thought the Rocket would score today if he was playing.

"About 25 or 30," said Harry.

"Is that all?"

"That's right, Dick," replied Harry. "Don't forget, he's sixty-four years old."

THE ROCKET BLASTS OFF

Some memories, opinions, thoughts, and occasionally cranky reflections from Rocket Richard:

On the toughness of hockey players today: "The game ain't as tough as it used to be. You can count on the fingers of less than two hands the really tough fighters in the game."

On how players in his era survived in the NHL: "Players in the NHL live by the Jungle Code. You have to make do the best way you know how."

On former NHL president Clarence Campbell: "He was always very standoffish. He reminded me of members of the English aristocracy of Canada who tend to look down on the French-Canadians as second-class citizens."

More from the Rocket on Campbell: "I never really liked him as a person. He always struck me as snobbish. When you talked to him he would look somewhere else, not straight at you."

On playing in Chicago and New York: "For me, New York and Chicago were the worst cities. There were so many crazy kids and crazy guys who would come behind our bench before and after the games and taunt us."

GORDIE ON THE ROCKET, AND THE ROCKET ON GORDIE

"He used to be a whirlwind. Now he's just a whirlwind half the time."

—Gordie Howe, on the Rocket

"Howe is a better all-around player than I was, but I never thought he was too good a money player. I don't remember Howe scoring many game-winning goals. It always looked as though he would even be a greater player if he hustled more."

—Rocket Richard, on Gordie Howe

Rocket Richard: Unbiased Observer

A wonderful custom in hockey is picking the stars of the game. Three stars are chosen based on their play in that night's game. They make a brief appearance afterwards on the ice when their names are announced. After he retired from hockey, Rocket Richard picked the three stars for a Detroit-Montreal game, and explained his reasons thusly:

"Well, I chose Henri Richard not because he's my brother, but because he's always driving. He was always trying tonight and so he's my No. 1 star. Then I picked Jean Beliveau as the second star, because he's an inspiration to Montreal. Without him, they wouldn't have been in the game at all. I know some people will think I chose these two because they play for my old team. Well, it isn't true. Because as the third star I pick Gordie Howe. If it wasn't for his three goals the Red Wings wouldn't have won, 3–0."

Icy Perfection

Another fabled Montreal Canadien was the classy Jean Beliveau. He was a teammate of Rocket Richard's. "Maurice can't learn from lectures," said Frank Selke, then the general manager of the Canadiens. "He does everything by instinct and sheer power. Beliveau, on the other hand, is probably the classiest player I've ever seen. The difference between the two is simply this: Richard is an opportunitist, Beliveau is a perfectionist."

The lanky Beliveau was merely perfect on skates—"poetry in action," was how one writer described it—and on the streets of Montreal, they revered him like no other. "Jean Beliveau in Quebec is like Mickey Mantle and Joe DiMaggio in the United States," observed the author Leonard Shecter. "When Jean Beliveau walks down the street in Quebec the women smile, the men shake his hand, and the little boys follow him." When asked how he had signed the popular Beliveau to a contract for Montreal, general manager Selke smiled and said, "No secret. I simply opened the Forum vault and said, 'Help yourself, Jean.'"

HOWIE THE GREAT

Howie Morenz played in the 1920s, but he was as fast as Pavel Bure, a blur on the ice. "He's some wild wind, that No. 7," said goalie Roy Worters. "To me he's just a blur—7777777." Morenz was the first great star in the Montreal dynasty, a forerunner of Rocket Richard, Jean Beliveau, Guy Lafleur, Patrick Roy, and so many more. "When Howie skated full speed, everyone else on the ice seemed to be skating backwards," wrote one sportswriter. One story about Howie says that he came to a game drunk, but still scored three times. "I have a new scoring method," he joked. "First I breathe on the goalie, then I shoot it in!" After he died, one of his former teammates said, "Morenz was something that was only once." A most fitting eulogy for one of the game's early greats.

OLD-TIME HOCKEY TALK

Larry Zeidel once described himself as "the only Jewish guy in hockey who doesn't own a team." Larry was a 39-year-old nobody with the expansion Philadelphia Flyers. He was not a great player, nor was he very good. But he did score a goal for those Flyers, on New Year's Eve in the first year of the team's existence. "Every time I score a goal for the Flyers, it's like New Year's Eve," Larry said with a laugh. It was the only goal he scored in his brief shot at NHL glory.

Defenseman Rod Seiling likened Phil Esposito to "a damned tree" when he planted himself in front of the opposition net. Boston fans in the sixties and seventies had a great bumper sticker back then: "JESUS SAVES—BUT ESPO SCORES ON THE REBOUND!" . . . A journeyman named Brian Smith seldom scored on the rebound, or any other way. Between periods in one game he started skating on the ice with the Zamboni machine. "What the hell are you doing?" a teammate wanted to know. "Don't you see?" said Smith. "This is my way of getting on TV."

When asked who he thought was going to win Rookie of the Year honors for the 1951–52 season, Boom Boom Geoffrion answered, "Me." He was right. . . . Back in the forties, a young rookie asked Bucko McDonald—now *there's* a name for you—how to make it in the NHL. "Keep your head up, and get your hair cut," he said. . . . Tom Lysiak, who played for the Flames in the 1970s, had a different technique for NHL survival: "What I've learned is that whatever you do in hockey, you should cheat at it. Everyone cheats in hockey. It's unbelievable how much you can get away with—if you do it when no one is looking, of course." Of course.

The New York Islanders were leading the Canadiens late in a playoff game. But Montreal came back to score two third-period goals, tie the New Yorkers in regulation, and then beat them in overtime. Eddie Westfall of the Isles said it was "like having two spares in the trunk and winding up with three flats." . . . The Isles as a team must have felt a little like beleaguered Vic Hadfield, when he was the lone New York Ranger defending against a 3-on-1 break. "Spread out, Vic," his teammates yelled at him, "spread out!"

10

THE INTERNATIONAL GAME

Hockey is Canada's game, right? Well, not anymore. "People have a tough time dealing with it," says Winnipeg general manager Mike Smith. "But the fact is, it hasn't been Canada's game since 1972." That was the year Canadian hockey stars from the NHL met the Russians for the first time in international competition, and although Team Canada won that series—by a margin as thin as an ice shaving—those matches changed the game forever. Hockey has become an international phenomenom that is played in Russia, Europe, and even—and this may be the most astonishing fact of all—in parts of the American West and Southeast. Here's a look at how far the game has come since 1972:

THE SERIES

The most famous hockey matches of all time occurred in 1972, when a team of NHL stars met the Soviet Union in an incredibly dramatic, emotion-wracked series. Canadian pros have played Russian and European teams many times since, but nothing can ever match what was at stake in those eight games played in cities across Canada and Moscow nearly thirty-five years ago. Canada won with a Paul Henderson goal with 34 seconds left to play in the eighth game, salvaging what was left of her national pride. But the play of the Russians, and their shocking dominance of the NHL stars in the first four games in Canada, shook the hockey world like an earthquake. Hockey had been an Olympic sport for decades, but this was something different, very different. The marvelously skilled Russian team showed that you didn't have to be Canadian to play Canada's game, and in so doing gave birth to a truly international sport.

Reading the Canadian press clips prior to that 1972 series is to go back to a simpler, more innocent time, at least in hockey terms. There was simply no way the Canadians could lose—*no way*. But they weren't just going to beat the Russians, it was going to be a bloody massacre, a frightful thing to watch. Hide the women and children. "National pity prepared to light candles for the Soviet Union," as novelist Jack Ludwig put it. If there was one Canadian alive who believed the USSR had a chance to score a goal, much less win a game—be serious!—he must have been living under a bridge somewhere in Nova Scotia. "8–0 Canada," predicted one sportswriter. "And that's also the score of the first game." Dick Beddoes, another writer, put in his two cents: "Canada to romp in eight. It's a Russian team in decay."

The players—the best from the NHL—were equally cocky. "No goalie should have any trouble against them," said Jacques Plante, who wasn't on the team but who was confident anyway. "It's their whole team. Everything they do is slower—passing, shooting, making plays. They're not used to playing against this kind of competition—and they won't be able to keep pace." Asked how he thought the Russians would do, Yvan Cournoyer said, "I don't know. I've never seen them play." But Fred Shero had seen them play and he knew, like so many other knowledgeable hockey people, how to stop them. "Don't follow all that fancy looping and circling they do," he advised. "You just stand up at the blue line, because despite all the looping and circling, eventually they'll have to come to you."

The Canadian press judged the Soviet goalie, Vladislav Tretiak, as "weak." (Tretiak was weak the way Hercules was weak.) The Russian defense was "suspect" and in recent international matches, the squad had "failed to impress." Canadians were rubbing their hands together in collective glee. "Bobrov's Bobcats will become Pavlov's Kittens," chortled columnist Ted Blackman. Alan Eagleson, head of the NHL Players Association and one of the organizers of the event, said, "Anything less than an unblemished sweep of the Russians would bring shame down on the heads of the players and the national pride." Ah, but what's to worry? It'll be a cakewalk, 8–0 or at worst, 7–1. Every Maple Leaf–loving man, woman, and child felt as Bobby Clarke did, and knew in their hearts it was true: "We're finally getting a chance to prove that we are what we believe," said Clarke. "The best hockey players in the world." Pity the poor Russians.

GAMES 1–4: THE CANADIAN GAMES

Pity the poor Canadians.

The first game occurred on September 2, 1972, in Montreal. The Soviet Union won, 7–3. The next day was a national day of mourning in Canada. People were stunned. It was as if the sun had decided, on a whim, not to rise that day. All across Canada, in gloomy darkened rooms, hockey fans were being forced to eat plates of crow. Even worse than the loss, if there could be something worse than losing, was the way in which Canada's boys had gone down to ignominious defeat. The team had acted like spoiled, hotheaded brats. "As if Armageddon weren't bad enough," explained Jack Ludwig, "the team had turned into nothing but a bunch of rinkrats and rednecks." As early as the second period, Team Canada had begun to resort to "chippy bush-league tricks" in trying to slow down the Russians, who turned out to be much faster and cleverer than anyone had foreseen. Afterward the humiliated Canadians didn't even shake hands with the Russians, although some of the Canadians said they weren't aware they were supposed to. The *Toronto Star* called the team "bush-league soreheads." Scott Young wrote, "The thing that shamed me, and I guess many of us, was not the loss. That was nothing—one team playing hockey at its best and deserving to win. But when grown Canadians wearing their nation's name on their backs get chippy, cheaply chippy, I feel badly for us. The night when we show that we can't dish it out, we can't take it either."

The recriminations began immediately. "Has the NHL been perpetrating a fraud all these years, by claiming the world's best hockey?" asked Dick Beddoes, who had earlier predicted a Canadian sweep. Milt Dunnell of the *Toronto Star* joined in the bashing. "How would you like to lay out $200,000 per season for the world's greatest hockey players by admission of their lawyers, and then see them get clobbered, 7–3, by a bunch of guys named Yuri, Vladimir, and Eugeni who are drawing lance corporals' pay?" he wrote. A Canadian Olympic official blamed the stodginess of hockey coaches and their unwillingness to teach different ways of playing the game. "Our coaching technique in hockey hasn't changed in twenty-five years," said Aubrey Hillhouse. "We've stood still, refusing to believe there are better ways to play our national game."

Team Canada won the second game, 4–1, but there was more criticism of its rough style of play—criticism that would continue throughout the series. Wayne Cashman came under attack for his repeated attacks on the Russian skaters. "What's he trying to do, prove his manhood? Or his boyhood?" said one critic. The team was derided as "Team NHL" or "Team U.S.-NHL," because of the decision to keep World Hockey Association stars like Bobby Hull off the team. Hull had jumped to the Winnipeg Jets of the rival WHA, and the old-line NHL establishment had blackballed him from the team. "As an old hockey man," said Conn Smythe, an old hockey man, "I am proud there are no contract breakers representing our country." Shouts of "Where's Bobby Hull?" followed the team across the country.

Game 3, in Winnipeg, ended in a 4–4 tie. In Game 4 the Russians won again, 5–3, and fans in Vancouver actually booed their national team. Milt Dunnell wrote, "Last night, as the last air escaped from the punctured balloon of a national ego, it had the angry sound of disappointment, disillusionment, and, excuse the word, contempt." The contempt arose from the continuing roughhouse tactics of the Canadians, notably an incident in which Frank Mahovlich mugged Vladislav Tretiak in the goal. The members of Team Canada could not fail to hear the booing, and they reacted defensively. "Do these people think we're some kind of dishonorable men who just hit people for no reason?" said defenseman Brad Park. Eric Whitehead of the *Vancouver Province* said the fans were mad not just at the players but at "the fat and happy NHL establishment that has been content to sit back and just rake in the money while the skills of the game have gone to pot." He added, "It is already plain that the upstart Soviets play a sounder, better, and more exciting hockey than is seen in the NHL."

At the end of four games the Russians had won two and the Canadians one, with one tie. Whitehead described it as a "long week of humiliation." As the series shifted to Moscow for the final four games, while Canada suffered a national identity crisis, new respect emerged for the Russian team. Their precision passing and team play were teaching lessons to the country that invented the game. "Size does not make the Canadians strong or give them ability," said Aleksandr Yakushev, one of the Soviet stars. "If you have too many big players, then your team is slow." The Canadians did not agree with that analysis, but they conceded that the Russians were good—very good. "The Russians compare with any team in the NHL," said Harry Sinden, coach of Team Canada. "Anybody in this country who thinks we're not playing a great hockey team is crazy. I haven't seen any Russians who couldn't play in the NHL," Sinden added. The man they booed in Vancouver, Frank Mahovlich, agreed. "Listen," he said, "give those Russians a football and in three years they'd beat the Dallas Cowboys."

GAMES 5–8: THE GOAL OF THE CENTURY

Upon arriving in Moscow for the final four games of the series, Harry Sinden was asked what he was going to do after they were over. "Hide," he said. Fortunately for Sinden and his players, they didn't have to hide their heads after all. But it was close—very, very close.

Before the matches in Russia began the Canadians flew to Sweden to practice. Dissension split the ranks. Upset over his poor treatment and lack of playing time, Vic Hadfield, captain of the New York Rangers, quit the team and flew home. So did Gil Perreault and two others. Their coach was not pleased. "Hadfield wasn't playing well enough to make the squad that dressed for games," said Sinden, who was furious at the players for leaving. "I'd like to make them walk back to Canada myself," he said. "They aren't man enough to stand up and say they wanted out of the moral commitment to Team Canada because things looked gloomy." But Sinden himself was under attack for the team's poor performance, as were many of the players. "Ken Dryden identified himself as one of the best goalkeepers in the world," noted Jack Ludwig. "After his two games in Canada that evaluation qualified as delusion." A cartoon appearing in Canadian papers at the time portrayed the national mood. It shows two kids trading hockey cards. One of them says, "What about a Ken Dryden, three Bobby Clarkes, two Yvan Cournoyers, two Paul Hendersons, a Phil Esposito and seventeen Vic Hadfields for your Vikulov?" Vikulov was one of the Russian stars and the kid holding his card isn't taking.

Russia won the opening game in Moscow, 5–4. The Canadians

came back to win Game 6 by a score of 3–2. Still, their victory was tainted by their now-obvious strategy of physical intimidation and on-the-edge rough play. In Game Six, Team Canada received a bench penalty for "ugliness." Even the writers for one of the most repressive regimes in human history referred to some of the Canadian players as *nekulturny*, which is Russian for "uncultured" or "ill-mannered." People remembered why Phil Esposito used to be called "Dirty Phil" when he played for the Blackhawks. Wayne Cashman threw a violent check on a Russian player who had skated across the center line to track down the puck. Cashman shrugged it off. "The guy was in the wrong place," he said. "He should have known better."

If Team Canada was on a safari, it was clear who they were hunting: the great Soviet star, Valeriy Kharlamov. And eventually the Canadians got their man, as coach Sinden later admitted in his book: "Kharlamov, the Russian star, had been injured in the sixth game of the series, when his ankle jumped up and tried to assault (Pat) Whitey Stapleton's hockey stick. He missed the last game, but the Russians were pulling out all the stops for this one. In minutes, word came back that Kharlamov was getting a shot of Novocain and would be on the ice. 'I don't want any of you guys to go out of your way,' I told the players, 'but if he happens to skate by, and gets in your way, give him a tickle.'" If this "tickling" of Kharlamov had occurred on the street and not in a hockey arena, the players who did it might have been arrested. After the seventh game, won again by Team Canada, Russian assistant coach Boris Kulagin said: "Canadian players have forgotten the game is played under international rules."

But the Soviets were hardly innocent lambs. The officiating, as so often occurred in international sporting events during those Cold War days, seemed to favor the home team. Sinden jumped all over the referees, calling them "incompetent" and saying it was "the worst officiating I've ever seen in my life." The Soviets also received criticism for *their* style of play, which, said the Canadians, intentionally interfered with theirs. "Do you teach your players interference, Mr. Kulagin?" one Canadian sportswriter asked.

In the end, what it came down to was desire. The Canadians wanted to win as badly as human beings can want anything in this life, and their Russian opponents matched them shot for shot. At the rink in Moscow, a marching song entitled "Cowards Don't Play Hockey" accompanied the appearance of the Soviet team onto the ice. There were no cowards on the ice that last night. With Canadian fans chanting "*Da, da,* Canada, *Nyet, nyet,* Soviet" in the arena in Moscow, they played the eighth and final game. Team Canada came back from the dead to score three goals and knot the game at five apiece. Then, with the final seconds ticking down, Paul Henderson shot a rebound shot that the wondrous Russian goalie, Tretiak, fended off. But Henderson stayed home and slipped the puck into the net for a 6–5 Canada win. "No one who saw that final game or even listened to it on the radio will ever forget Paul Henderson's goal," writes Brian McFarlane. "It was the goal of the century." Canada had won the series, 4–3–1, and it set off a celebration across that vast and wondrous land.

Years later, McFarlane asked Tretiak about that goal, and this is what he said: "I think the Lord himself gave that goal to Henderson. It was a beautiful goal and a great surprise. Seconds earlier, Paul had fallen down behind the net, and I didn't even notice him. Do I dream about that goal? I can say with a smile, I think about it every day of my life."

THE AFTERMATH

So what did Henderson's goal mean? Everything, and nothing. Canada erupted into a nationwide celebration, her joy mixed with the most profound sort of relief. Happiest of all may have been the Canadians on hand in Moscow to witness that historic eighth

game. They took over an entire hotel, partying till the wee hours
with their somewhat more reserved Russian hosts looking on with
studied indifference. "You know what they're afraid of," said one
Canadian reveler. "The last party like this was called a revolu-
tion."

Across Canada, people shouted "We're Number One! We're
Number One!" and seemed to believe it. As one reporter pointed
out, Team Canada won by a single goal in the 480th minute of
play; that hardly justified a claim of global hockey supremacy.
"Our capacity for self-delusion seems limitless," wrote Jim Kear-
ney of the *Vancouver Sun*. Boris Kulagin, the besieged Russian
coach, handled himself with grace, conceding that the Canadians
won the last three games because they played better hockey.

The series generated worldwide comment. *Time* magazine re-
ferred to the boorish Canadian players as "adolescents on the last
frontier." On the same subject, one *New York Times* reporter
joked that "the only good thing about it is it's not being done by
Americans." Some inevitable anti-American sentiment did sur-
face during the series. Following Canada's stunning loss in the
opening game in Montreal, the *Toronto Star* editorialized in this
fashion:

"Instead of blaming our side for inept play, let us reflect a little on what Team Canada's humiliating loss to the Soviets tells us
about ourselves as Canadians. First, about our capacity for self-
delusion. Seldom since Goliath contemptuously looked at David
can an opponent have been so grossly underrated as we underrated the Soviets." Then, the *Star* cuts to the heart of the matter:
"But there is probably a more fundamental reason for Team
Canada's deficiencies. The rampant commercialization of hockey
in North America . . . The NHL All-Stars are representing this
country by the grace and favor of fourteen American clubowners.
We deluded ourselves by supposing that we could sell our national game—like our national economy—to the highest bidders
and still excel in our own right."

The *Star* concluded, "If Team Canada loses, let us not accuse it of letting Canada down. In its shortcomings, as in the 'Owned in U.S.A.' brand on most of its players, it probably represents us all too faithfully."

If Team Canada had lost, the *Star* argued, blame greedy American commercialism. But when the Canadians won, did the *Star* run another editorial praising those fourteen American clubowners and U.S. entrepreneurial capitalism? No, probably not. Montreal sportswriter John Robertson may have written the best analysis of the series. When all is said and done, said Robertson, we're just talking about hockey after all.

Wrote Robertson: "We didn't really win anything! We merely salvaged something from the wreckage—something to cling to, so we can say to the world: Well, we may be obnoxious barbarians; we may have come across as the most grotesque, uncouth people ever turned loose in an international athletic forum; we may have undone just about everything our diplomats abroad have been able to do for Canada's image; we may have shown the world we have absolutely no respect for game officials, opposing coaches, or the laws and customs in countries in which we are guests; we may lead the league in both menacing and obscene gestures; but," Robinson concludes—and this is really the nub of the matter—"at least we won the damned hockey game."

THE NHL VS. THE WORLD

The 1972 series was the first, but certainly not the last, time that NHL players faced the Soviets in high-stakes international hockey matches. Here are highlights from two other matches:

The Bullies Do Their Thing

In 1976, the Philadelphia Flyers—the Broad Street Bullies—whipped the Russians in an exhibition game. This was Bully hockey at its finest—or worst, depending on your point of view—

and the Russians walked off the ice at one point to protest the violent play. They later returned to the ice to get pummeled some more by Dave Schultz, Bobby Clarke and Co.

Appalled by the performance of the Flyers in a match supposedly designed to foster international goodwill, Robin Herman of the *New York Times* called it "the most vicious sports event I have ever seen." This made Flyers broadcaster Gene Hart flip a wig: "Do you know what you are?" he said the next time he saw Herman. "You're a dimwit. Why the hell don't you go write about a sport you know? The most vicious sports event you have ever seen? How many sports events have you seen? Six?" So much for international goodwill. . . .

Mario Makes His Mark

One of the best-ever matches between Russia and Canada occurred in the 1987 Canada Cup. The matches featured a three-game final and on the Canadian side, Mario Lemieux and Wayne Gretzky. The teams split the first two games, with Lemieux getting a hat trick in Team Canada's 6–5 double-overtime win in Game 2.

Game 3 was even better. For the first time in the series, Gretzky and Lemieux played on the same line together. Even so, Team Canada trailed 3–0 until things started to click. And how. Gretzky garnered five assists and Lemieux scored three goals for the second straight game, his last one the game-winner with 1:24 left in the third period. The Great One flipped a pass to Lemieux, who drove a shot past Sergei Mylnikov in the Soviet goal to make it 6–5, which was the final score. The series was a turning point in the career of Lemieux, who set a Canada Cup scoring record with 11 goals. Previously, critics—including Don Cherry—had called him "a floater," saying he couldn't handle the big games. "I think I've answered a few questions about myself in this tournament," said Mario in the locker room after the game. Indeed.

MIRACLE ON ICE

For United States hockey, 1980 is comparable to 1972 for Canada. That was the year a young American team beat the Russians in hockey at the Winter Olympics. (Though let us never forget that a similarly underrated U.S. team won the gold medal at Squaw Valley in 1960.) Many Americans remember Mike Eruzione's goal in the semifinals at Lake Placid the way Canadians remember Paul Henderson's in Moscow. Although the '72 Canadians were highly favored at the outset, in contrast to the '80 Americans, both goals accomplished the same thing: They beat the Russians.

Dan Jenkins wrote, "Hockey leaves Canada every four years to go to the Winter Olympics, but nobody knows it's there unless the United States beats Russia." In 1980 the United States beat Russia in hockey, and just about everybody in the country knew about it. "Do you believe in miracles?" the broadcaster Al Michaels asked, and even the most jaded sports fans had to answer with a resounding "Yes!" Even the American players were thunderstruck by what they had done: "I can't believe we beat them," said Mark Johnson, who scored two goals against the Russians in the 4–3 U.S. win. "I can't believe we beat them." The Russians, remember, were a team of paid professionals. They had been playing together in the Red Army for years. They were indisputably one of the finest hockey teams in the history of the game. They won everything there was to win in international hockey, and they did it in dominating fashion. They featured one of the greatest goalies in the history of the game, Vladislav Tretiak, on a team that could have challenged for the Stanley Cup title, if it had played in the NHL.

The U.S. players were exceptional hockey players too, but individually at least, they did not match up with the Russians. Who could? The Americans were *amateurs,* for crying out loud, a ragtag band of college guys who saw the Olympics as a showcase for potential NHL careers. The coach who brought them together was Herb Brooks, who was about as friendly as a hockey stick in the eye. "He treated us all the same," said a member of the U.S. team. "Rotten." Brooks, said the writer E.M. Swift, was "as sentimental as a stone." Brooks resembled granite, because he wanted to win, and he wanted his players to win as badly as he did. "I'd hate to meet him in a dark alley," said the actor Karl Malden, who played Brooks in a TV movie that was made about the team. "I think he's a little on the neurotic side. Maybe more than a little. Any moment you think he's going to jump out of his skin."

Brooks's coaching style boiled down to this: "He pats you on the back but always lets you know he has the knife in the other hand." Buzz Schneider, who played for Brooks on that Olympic team and for three years at the University of Minnesota, said that. Another player who played at both Minnesota and on the '80 team, Phil Verchota, said that when you said "Hi" to Brooks, sometimes he wouldn't even answer "Hi" back. "I can remember times when I was so mad at him I tried to skate so hard I'd collapse," said Dave Silk, a member of the U.S. team. "So I could say to him, 'See what you did.'" What Brooks did, in the end, was unite his players against an even more formidable opponent than him, the Russians.

But the Americans did not capture the imagination of their countrymen because they were robots, automatically following the orders of their over-programmed coach. Mike Eruzione was their leader and captain. Jim Craig was the outstanding goalie who skated across the ice looking for his dad after the gold medal win over Finland. These two stood out on a team that, as a whole, had great personality and verve. And as the Americans climbed their improbable way up the Olympic beanstalk, a lot of people who knew nothing about hockey started to care about them . . . a great deal. "Norway . . . Romania . . . West Germany, down they went, each game a struggle in the early going, pulled out in the third period when those kids who looked about fifteen simply blew the opposition away," writes E.M. Swift. "And afterward the players would line up at center ice and smile those great big wonderful smiles, many of which actually displayed teeth, and salute the fans." Fans all across the country saluted back, and a great love affair was born.

Then came the Russians. Brooks, for one, thought they were ripe for the taking—or, as he says so much more expressively: "The Russians were ready to cut their own throats." Still, the Americans had to be willing to take advantage. Okay, Brooks is more vivid on this point too: "But we had to get to the point to be ready to pick up the knife and hand it to them," he says. The Americans were ready with the cutlery—"Here, try this well-sharpened butcher knife, Mr. Tretiak"—and cut the vaunted Soviet team to pieces. After the U.S. beat the Russians, the Finns—in the gold-medal game—were so much shish kebab to the Americans.

"Your victory was one of the most breathtaking upsets, not only in Olympic history but in the entire history of sports," President Jimmy Carter told the U.S. players when they visited the White House, and you know something? Jimmy was right.

TEAM MEDIOCRE

Unlike 1980, the 1994 Olympics in Norway was not America's finest hockey hour. While Sweden was winning the gold, beating Canada in a thrilling shootout, Team USA went down quickly and meekly, finishing a lowly eighth. In retrospect the American team should have followed Michael Ventre's advice: "If I'm the head of the USOC, I let Tonya Harding go to Lillehammer. I think our hockey team could use some muscle." Some candid assessments of "Team Mediocre," as it was called, and its performance in the Norway games:

If the NHL allows its top stars to play in the Olympics, Sergei Fedorov could play for Russia and try to restore his country's international hockey reputation. Photo courtesy of the Detroit Red Wings

"It will be very difficult for them to beat us. This team is motivated and hungry right now. I have said too much, but I don't care."

> —Finland coach Curt Lindstrom, prior to facing Team USA in the Olympic tournament

"We let those guys take the stupid penalties. It's always that way [against the Americans]. Those guys are a little bigger. They always try to intimidate Europeans. We knew that we are a better team if we play our game, let them push around, do that kind of junk."

> —Finland's Mika Nieminen, commenting on the USA's physical style after the Finns dispatched the Americans, 6–1

"These U.S. guys are trying to get there [to the NHL]. We've got guys who have been there."
> —Mikko Maekelae, also of Finland who has played in the NHL

"They're a bunch of divers. They're a disgrace to their country."
> —Slovakia's Peter Stastny, claiming that the American players faked penalties by flopping on the ice. (Slovakia and the U.S. tied 3–3.)

"If a tie is like kissing your sister, we can only assume a hockey tie with France is like French–kissing your sister."
> —Sportswriter Bob Kravitz, on Team USA's 4–4 tie with France

"'This team never quits,' center Todd Marchant said. Now, if it can just start winning."
> —John Crumpacker, sportswriter

"There will be no 'Miracle on Ice' this time around. There won't even be a Darn Nice Try."
> —Unidentified sportswriter

Post Mortem on Team USA

There's no sense kicking a dead dog . . . aw, what the heck, let's kick it a little bit. Team USA tried hard in '94, but this group of collegians and sometime-pros just couldn't cut it against the Swedens and Canadas of the world. Much of the criticism for the team's poor performance fell on head coach Tim Taylor, the Yale hockey coach. "The players took their emotional cues from him," wrote Helene Elliott of the *Los Angeles Times*. "And Taylor stood there, barking commands with an expressionless face, arms folded across his chest." After the U.S. took a 1–0 lead on eventual gold-medal winner Sweden in a preliminary round game, "the U.S. players should have been flying," says Elliott. "When they went flat instead, Taylor did nothing to rekindle the fire. Not a pat on the back, not a 'Keep it going, guys,' not a smile."

The American players rallied around the stoical Taylor. "The coaches put in so much effort, and we let them down," said goalie Garth Snow. "Our coaches are too nice of guys to get treated the way they did in this tournament." Nice guy or not, Taylor knew how his team would be judged and said so: "You have to keep the perspective that we had a great season and we did a lot of tremendous things on the ice and off the ice. We just didn't get the job done hockeywise, and if that's the only measure of their success and failure, we have to be labeled a failure."

HOCKEY DREAM TEAMS?

The 1994 Olympic hockey tournament was one of the weakest ever, in large part because the best hockey players in the world were playing in the NHL. For future Olympics the NHL will likely take a break from its regular season and allow its players to play on "Dream Teams" for their respective countries. Not everyone, however, thinks this is a good idea, or that it will stimulate renewed interest in Olympic hockey. Some opinions from the debate:

"I don't think [the Olympics] should be an exercise in some sort of vacation from their regular season. To come over and play eight games, then go back to their regular season, I don't like that idea. I don't think that's what the Olympics are all about and I think something would be lost from Olympic competition if that happened."

—Tim Taylor, 1994 Team USA coach

"For the development of hockey, I think the best players in the world should be here. Most of the top players are in the NHL, so

that's the way I hope it will be in the future. Real hockey people want to see the best."
                                          —Carl Lindstrom, Finland hockey coach

"For the Olympics, the NHL players would add some prestige to what has become a watered-down event marked by lackluster play and the absence of a Goliath for all those Davids to shoot at."
                                          —Michael Farber, sportswriter

"People say they want it, but if the U.S. Dream Team didn't do well, there probably wouldn't be much of a response. Olympic fans watch Olympic hockey, but that doesn't mean they'll watch the NHL."
                                          —Sandy Grossman, TV sports director

"I'd like to find a solution. I look at my son. He's wearing a Chicago Bulls jacket, and I'm president of the Swiss Ice Hockey Federation. Why? Because of the Dream Team and all that stuff. Now nobody's interested in this [Olympic] tournament."
                                          —Rene Fasel, a Swiss representative on
                                          the International Ice Hockey Federation

THE RISE AND FALL OF RUSSIAN HOCKEY

You think times are tough for American hockey? Think about the Russians. They used to be the Tyrannosaurus Rex of international hockey; now they can't even beat Barney. Okay, okay, they still can whip the pants off the United States in hockey—big deal. The old Soviet Union athletic machine is no more, and many of the best Russian players have come to the NHL. A contributor to Herb Caen's column in the *San Francisco Chronicle*, while watching the NHL playoffs, joked that "it's just a matter of whether *our* Russian hockey players are better than *their* Russian hockey players." That's an exaggeration—there are Swedes and Finns and, oh yes, some Canadians mixed in there too—but it's still a far cry

from the days when the Soviet Union was the Big Red Menace
of the international game.

With people like Pavel Bure and Sergei Fedorov possibly on
the team, Russia will do just fine when top NHL players start
playing in the Olympics. But in 1994 that wasn't the case, and the
Unified Team really suffered. "What's the world coming to when
the Russian hockey team resorts to amateur talent in Olympic
competition?" chuckled sportswriter Bud Geracie. In the past
they used to air-express the gold medal to the Russians before
the Olympics even started. In 1994 the Unifieds did not come
close to winning the gold, and worse, they suffered a 5–0 shel-
lacking at the hands of their uppity neighbors, Finland. "It was a
humiliation of Russian hockey, that game," said Igor Larionov.
"That was sad to watch. You can lose, but not like that. It was a
disaster."

Larionov, currently a star for the San Jose Sharks and one of
dozens of Russians in the NHL, played for the great Soviet Union
teams of the 1980s. He and teammates Sergei Makarov—also
starring for the Sharks—Vladimir Krutov and others used to kick
butt and takes names, as they say. The Soviet Union won gold
medals in 1984 and 1988 and as the Unified Team, again in 1992.
Until 1994, the only gold medals not won by the Soviets in the
past ten Olympic Games were the two won by the USA in their
"miracle" upsets of 1960 and 1980. Arturs Irbe, goalie for the
Sharks who played against the Soviets while a resident of his native Latvia, remembers what it was like to come up against Larionov, Makarov and Co. "They never got more than 8 against me,"
laughed Irbe. "They were just awesome." Just keeping the Soviets under 10 goals in a game was an achievement for a goalie.

The coach of those teams was Viktor Tikhonov, the Woody
Hayes of Soviet hockey. He ran those teams like the little dicta-
tor he was, and produced results. This did not necessarily endear
him to his players. The great star Larionov said that Tikhonov
"treated me like a pig." Larionov points out that while Tikhonov
was a good coach, he had good players, too. *Very* good players.

In 1994, when most of the good Russian players were off in the NHL, Tikhonov did not fare so well. It is players' being in creative harmony with a system that makes for winning teams, not a system alone. "I feel sorry for the boys," said Larionov after the Finnish disgrace of the Russian team in 1994, "because it's hard to play when the coach is screaming from the bench. He [Tikhonov] has no success anymore, but he's still demanding the same thing." A recipe for failure in any sport, in any country.

CHECKING OUT THE OTHER WINTER SPORTS

Who says hockey is a rough sport? Tony Kornheiser of the *Washington Post* checked out the scene at the last Olympics and filed this report:

"Moguls-aerials—leaping into the air and doing whirly-gigs on skis, what are you, nuts? You could break your head.

"Ski jumping—palpably insane, off the charts.

"Downhill skiing—going straight down the mountain, are you kidding me?

"Bobsled—you think that tin crate is going to save you?

"Luge—on your back, on a pie plate at 80 miles per hour, good luck.

"Biathlon—they're using real bullets . . . The safest sport in the Winter Olympics is hockey!"

11

FANS

Where would hockey be without its fans? Well, there'd be a lot of empty seats, for one. And without people in the seats, who'd be around to throw hats on the ice when somebody scored three goals? Not to mention octopi. Hockey fans, like the game itself, are changing. Hockey used to be a game played and watched by working-class and middle-class people. Nowadays ticket prices are so high that you need to take a second mortgage on your home to afford to go to an NHL game. Even with all the changes, hockey fans remain true to their game and love it more than ever.

A PARTIAL LIST OF THINGS THAT HOCKEY FANS HAVE THROWN ONTO THE ICE

Dead fish
Coins
Fruit of all types, particularly tomatoes
Beer (either poured or in cups)
Cans (tin and aluminum)
Boxing gloves (during a big Canucks-Leafs brawl)

Iron bolts
Bricks
Wood blocks
Firecrackers
Chairs
Armrests of chairs
Seat cushions
Toilet paper
Peanuts
Ink bottle
Marbles
Lightbulbs
Programs
Rotten eggs
Live chicken (at a Los Angeles Kings game, dressed in
   purple and gold, then the Kings' colors)
Dead turkey
Dead rabbit
Squid
Octopi (Detroit's immortal contribution to hockey lore)
Three pigs (at Quebec City)
Toe rubbers
Hats
Sugar packets (Ranger fans threw these at the diabetic
   Bobby Clarke of the Flyers)
45 rpm phonograph record (whistling by the head of the
   Rangers' Brad Park, in a visit to Boston Garden)
Water bottles
Cigarette lighter
Lit cigarettes
Rubber chicken
Puck with string attached to it (when the linesman bent
   down to pick it up, the fan would pull it and make the
   linesman chase after it)
Trash of all types

Easter bonnets
Cherry bombs
Soft drinks
Confetti
Trailer hitch
Batteries
Galoshes
Girdles
Beefsteaks
Buttons
(Author's note: The preceding list is merely reportorial in
    nature and not intended to give hockey fans any ideas.)

How to Throw an Octopus

The octopus is hockey's most fabled sea creature. The octopus is
unique. There is nothing like it in any other sport. Along with
Gordie Howe, it is Detroit's eternal contribution to sports and
hockey lore. The Father of Octopus Throwing, Pete Cusimano,
first did it in a 1952 playoff game at Detroit's old Olympia Stadium. Cusimano's family was in the fish and poultry business, and
Pete brought an octopus to the game and threw it onto the ice to
give the Red Wings good luck. Since then it has become a regular staple of Detroit home games. "Imagine some Detroit Red
Wings fans getting ready to go to a game," says Dave Einstein.
"'Let's see—we've got the tickets . . . the binoculars . . . oh, and
who's got the octopus?'"

If you're ever in Detroit at a game and the person next to you
needs some help in throwing his octopus, here's how one Red
Wings fan explained how to do it: "If you're trying to throw an
octopus raw, it tends to get away from you. It's slippery. It has-
n't got any bones or anything. If you boil it the octopus shrivels
up a bit and you can get a handle on it. Even so, you have to
sling the octopus stiff-armed and kind of sideways, like tossing

a hand grenade." He adds, noting the biggest drawback to octopus pitching: "It's hard to throw an octopus with pinpoint ac-
curacy."

SHARKS FAN GIVES HER ALL

A new chapter in the ancient custom of throwing things at hockey
games occurred on March 29, 1994, at the San Jose Arena. A
woman peeled off her bra and threw it onto the ice. The Sharks
were playing Winnipeg, and Sergei Makarov of the hometown
boys had just scored his third goal of the game. Caps cascaded
onto the ice along with—yes—the bra. *Sports Illustrated* re-
ported that it was "a frilly red bra, size 36C," and that it formerly
belonged to one Mari Ivener of Sunnyvale, California. Mari got
carried away with Sergei's feat and lacking a hat, threw the next
best thing. "It was a gorgeous red Victoria's Secret garment, perfect for Sergei the Red," she told a reporter. Even jaded hockey
writers, accustomed to dead fish and such things being hurled
onto the ice, took note of Mari's sacrifice. Said Bud Geracie: "A
red brassiere was thrown onto the ice after Sergei Makarov's
third goal Tuesday night. Stanley Cups?"

STEER LOSES HEAD OVER HOCKEY

At Colby College in Maine, students took a page out of *The Godfather* and threw the head of a steer onto the ice at a game. Okay,
okay, it was a horse's head in *The Godfather,* but maybe there
weren't any horses available to those fun-loving students at Colby.
At any rate, they had to stop the game for over an hour while work-
men cleaned up the ice. But the cleanup job wasn't that bad; apparently the head did not contain a great deal of residue. As Colby
sports information director Craig Cheslog explained, "It was red
and bloody, but it wasn't dripping."

GREAT TAUNTS

"Fifty years! Fifty years!"
> —The taunt from Islander fans at the rival New York Rangers, referring to the Rangers' inability to win a Stanley Cup since 1940

"Nineteen-forty! Nineteen-forty!"
> —A similar chant, heard in NHL arenas, mocking the Rangers (Of course, the Rangers put these chants forever to rest with their Stanley Cup victory in 1994)

"Get a sex change and become a man!"
> —New Yorker's taunt to a visiting player

"We got a place here in Massachusetts that's named after you. It's called Marblehead!"
> —A Bruin fan, yelling at an Islander goalie

"Send him a fax—it'll get there faster!"
> —Taunt at a player whose shot was blocked by the goalie

"There's a bus leaving for Oklahoma City at eleven o'clock. Be under it!"
> —A Red Wing fan, taunting an opposing player

"Who's your skating coach? Nancy Kerrigan? Stay on over. The Ice Follies come in tomorrow and you can earn an honest living."
> —Taunt at a smooth-skating European player

HOCKEY FANS OF YESTERYEAR

"Never before in the history of the game was such a crowd present or such enthusiasm evident. Tin horns, strong lungs and a general rabble predominated."

> —*Montreal Gazette*, describing the first-ever Stanley Cup match in 1894

"At the finish the spectators arose as one. From the boxes and upper benches rolled forth one great volume of sound. Both teams were carried off the ice."

> —1900 account of fan noise during a Stanley Cup match

"The outburst which greeted Bain's goal is beyond the power of the pen to describe. Half the people in the rink sat motionless with the word disappointment written all over their faces. The other half rose as one and broke into frantic cheers. Scores of them poured over the sides of the rink and carried the boys to their dressing room."

> —Reaction of Winnipeg fans to their team's 1901 Stanley Cup victory over Montreal

"The crowds threw off all restraint. They began to celebrate with a vengeance. It is a fact that wines of foreign vintage were in demand last night."

> —*Winnipeg Free Press*, heady over that same win

"With lungs of leather and throats of brass."

> —1902 description of how Montreal fans cheered their hockey team

AND NOW, HOCKEY FANS OF TODAY

New York Fans

"Sometimes you think those guys must have come out of the chimp cages at the Bronx Zoo."
> —Retired Boston goalie Gerry Cheevers, on New York fans

"It made me sick. I was scared. Don't those people know it's wrong? Don't they know they can hurt somebody? The crowd here is the worst in hockey. You should hear the filthy stuff they call us."
> —More from Cheevers on New York fans

"I'm a gracious winner. I'll call the New York fans sick animals and leave it at that. They are worth only two words."
> —Another Boston Bruin, Derek Sanderson, after they beat the Rangers in a tough series at Madison Square Garden

Philly Fans

"It's a hockey town that's good to get out of. There's always that twinge of fear when you're going in there: you're moving into the danger zone."
> —Hockey player, on visiting Philadelphia

"The goddamned people are nuts. They're out of their minds. If I had known this would happen, I would have rooted for the Bruins."
> —Philadelphia sportswriter, after a riot broke out in Philadelphia following the Flyers' first Cup win in 1974

*THE FANS INVOLVED IN THE FIGHT ARE ALIVE AND WELL. 18 BRU-
INS COULDN'T HURT THEM.*

> —Scoreboard message at the Philadel-
> phia Spectrum after several Boston Bruin
> players went into the stands to fight some
> fans during a Philly-Boston donnybrook

Boston Fans

*"All the [Boston] fans want are blood and guts. They throw
things. And the players are always running at you. This combina-
tion gives a visiting player the feeling he's a performer in the Ro-
man Coliseum."*

> —Brad Park, on being a visiting player
> at Boston Garden

*"A lot of outsiders have put down the Boston hockey fans, but
not me. I love Boston. I like the guys who come to the games with
two days' growth on their face, the gooks who scream their lungs
out. I love them because they're good people who work hard. They
never got a break in life, so their enjoyment is the hockey game.
For my money, hockey fans are the greatest in the world."*

> —Derek Sanderson, former Boston Bruin

Chicago Fans

*"The booing grew in volume until it seemed that we were caught
in a horrible miasma of hate and fury. The Hawks came out and
it was like an armada of roaring airplanes above the earth blotting
out the sky and the earth and human reason."*

> —Toronto reporter Andy Lytle, describ-
> ing a typical Blackhawks game at Chicago
> Stadium

*"Normally I try to ignore crowd reaction, but in Chicago it's
impossible. You can't help but get a lift from it."*

> —Bobby Hull

"Hockey's largest, noisiest and most rabid audience."
>—Visiting sportswriter Red Burnett, not as enamored of Chicago as Bobby was

"A hostile mob."
>—Montreal sportswriter, also not impressed with Chicago

"It's tough to play against the Hawks, three officials, and 20,000 fans."
>—Punch Imlach, Toronto coach

"Now I know what it's like to have people coming at me, ready to tear me apart. There were 20,000 people screaming for my blood. They hated my guts. How can so many people hate so much?"
>—Referee Red Storey, after he made a call against the Blackhawks

CITY OF WET BASEMENTS

Toronto is a wonderful city with a great hockey tradition, but "the City That Never Sleeps" it is not. "Toronto on a Sunday afternoon is about as dull as any place can be," noted a visiting sportswriter, D.A. MacDonald, a half-century ago. Times change, but apparently not Toronto. "It was such a trouncing," noted Scott Ostler during a 1994 playoff game there, "that half the fans in the Gardens had filed out and were enjoying the city's other favorite form of entertainment—watching the traffic light change." Ostler, who lives in San Francisco, has observed the differences between his city and Toronto. "Brief cultural comparison," he writes. "In this fine newspaper [*San Francisco Chronicle*] there is a regular advertisement for penile enlargement. A similar regular ad in the *Toronto Star's* sports section is headlined WET BASEMENTS?"

Ostler concludes that these "two forms of home improvement re-flect the priorities of the two regions."

Whether your interests run to wet basements or, well, other things, Toronto still has it all over another Canadian city, Win-nipeg. There's an old joke, and it still applies: "I spent a month in Winnipeg . . . last night."

Burnt Wings

Pity the poor Red Wings fan. His team is to the playoffs what the Titanic was to shipping. Mitch Albom, the Detroit columnist, knows full well the angst of being a fan of the Wings. Speaking in 1994 to his fellow sufferers (a year in which their team, naturally, went out early in the playoffs), Albom wrote, "Once upon a time you let this hockey team get to you. Like last season, when the Wings exited the playoffs in the first round, and you swore—what was it exactly?—that you would eat camel droppings before you'd go to another game."

Ah, but hope springs eternal in the hearts of Red Wing fans. They keep coming back, even if they know the fate that awaits them. "Remember 1991," said Albom, "another first round play-off exit? Or 1990, when they missed the playoffs altogether—even though missing the hockey playoffs is like missing the Atlantic Ocean in a boat?"

Red Wings fans always think the next season will be different, but it never is. "Now, admittedly," said Albom, "you thought this season might be different. The Wings had a new coach . . . and the most explosive offense in the game. And of course, they no longer had goalie Tim Cheveldae, whom you affectionately re-ferred to as 'Satan' after last year's playoffs." In 1994, however, the Wings had another problematic figure in goal, Chris Osgood. "Don't even mention Osgood," commanded Albom. "Two stinkin' shots, and he lets them both in. This kid can't even shave, and we're depending on him to save our necks?"

Well, Osgood didn't save their necks; nobody did. The Wings

lost in the playoffs, as they always somehow manage to do. So, for Albom and other Detroit fans, it's wait till next year—eternally, wait till next year—or look ahead to baseball. But that's sort of bleak too. Concluded Albom, ever the realist: "The next possible playoff game of any kind in this city would be baseball in October, and given the Tigers, we're talking October 2003."

SHARK FEVER

Expansion has its drawbacks, but one of the best things about it is when an area that's new to the game turns on to hockey and then flips out over it. That's hippie jargon for the nineties' phenomenon of the San Jose Sharks, who joined the NHL in 1991 and for two years should have been called "the Cow Palace Sharks," because they played their home games in a dilapidated former livestock arena on the outskirts of San Francisco. Those were bad years for the Sharks. About the only thing they had going for them was the coolest team logo in professional sports.

Then came the 1993–94 season. After losing seventy-one games the year before, the Sharks managed the biggest turnaround in league history and made the playoffs. The brand-new San Jose Arena opened, and the local citizenry went bananas. Billing itself as the capital of Silicon Valley, San Jose has long been in the shadow of its more glamorous and picturesque Bay Area neighbor, San Francisco. But the arrival of a professional hockey team gave San Jose an identity and a sense of civic pride it didn't have before. If you had asked most outsiders, "Do You Know the Way to San Jose?" as in the Dionne Warwick song, they would have said no. In the Sharks' 1994 playoff series against the Red Wings, a *San Jose Mercury News* reporter asked one Detroit resident to find San Jose on the map. "Is it near San Diego?" he asked. That was typical. The Associated Press even confused San Jose with San Diego in a wire story.

After the Sharks beat the Wings, however, many Detroit residents became painfully aware of San Jose and its hockey team. It was the same in Toronto, and here the clash of hockey cultures was even more evident. Toronto is one of the oldest and greatest hockey towns; they were playing hockey there when San Jose was still a bunch of fruit orchards. "The Leafs have closets full of old Stanley Cups," noted sportswriter Scott Ostler, "while the Sharks and their fans wouldn't know a Stanley Cup from a Ryder Cup or a Stanley Steamer."

Still, that was half the fun of it. "San Jose's fans have learned a lot about hockey," Ostler wrote on another occasion, "but they still haven't learned to boo the home team. It takes years of experience. If the Leafs ever get down six goals at Maple Leaf Gardens in this series, the crowd there will blow out the bass on your TV speaker." The San Jose fans were innocents, and they fell for their "Men of Teal" with the intensity of teenage sweethearts. They made large amounts of noise at San Jose Arena, they did "the Chomp" (mimicking jaws with their hands), and they grabbed up Shark merchandise with the fever of shoppers at a bargain-basement sale. One San Jose columnist proudly noted that while skiing in Europe, one of the young sons of Princess Diana was photographed wearing a ski cap with the Sharks logo.

Hockey-savvy Toronto was far less enamored of the Sharks and the way they played the game. San Jose's two leading players (along with Latvian goalie Arturs Irbe) were Igor Larionov and Sergei Makarov, two former stars of Soviet hockey. As a result the Sharks played slower, European-style hockey—a subject of great derision in Toronto and many parts of the NHL. "It's not hockey for the ages," joked one NHL-ite, "it's hockey for the aged." Toronto newspapers called it "boring," "lackluster," and "tedious." The Sharks were the "masters of the mundane" and "set the sleepy tone." ("Actually," said Scott Ostler in reply, "the Sharks should be flattered. When a Canadian describes you as lackluster, brother, you have reached an elite pinnacle of lackluster. They know whereof they speak.") Media commentators Don Cherry and Barry Melrose also put the knock on the San Jose style. Melrose called the Sharks "the Mahatma Gandhis of

hockey" because of their unwillingness to mix it up, a trademark
of the North American style played by Toronto. "To way-north
hockey fans the Sharks are not hockey players," explained Scott
Ostler. "They are Russian chess masters, sipping their Gatorade
with their pinkies extended."

But the Sharks defended themselves and their less confronta-
tional style of hockey. "If fighting is toughness, let's go to the San
Jose Boys Club and get two tough guys and put them on the ice,"
said Dean Lombardi, the director of hockey operations for San
Jose. "Toughness is playing in eerie situations." Nor did Kevin Constantine, the Sharks coach, think that his charges were playing
"boring" hockey. "Come out to San Jose and see whether the fans
there think we're boring. My responsibility is to those people. And
they seem to like the way we play." Sharks center Todd Elik added,
"I'd be glad to be boring if it means I can carry that Stanley Cup."

Elik and the Sharks did not get that chance in 1994, and it may
be a long time before they ever do. At least in that matchup, North

Darius Kasparaitis is a favorite target of "the Sign
Lady," who held up this
sign about him: KAS-
PARAITIS CAN BE CURED IN
OUR LIFETIME. Photo cour-
tesy of the New York Is-
landers

American hockey (Toronto) beat European hockey (San Jose), although the Gatorade-sipping Russian chess masters stretched
their more physical opponents to seven games. But what certainly
did happen in 1994 was that a city (San Jose) and a region (the
Bay Area) experienced the charms and excitement of hockey for
the first time, and they will never be quite the same again. During the playoffs the *Mercury News* interviewed one Boris Iofis, a
countryman of Sharks goalie Arturs Irbe, who had emigrated
from Latvia to the United States only eighteen months before.
Iofis was a big fan of Irbe's and the Sharks. "It is good for the Bay
Area that game is here," he said in his improving English. "What
did you do before?" Good question.

THE SIGN LADY

A Sharks fan known only as "the Sign Lady" has become a minor
celebrity at the San Jose Arena by composing some pretty witty
put-downs of visiting teams. Here is a sampling:

HEY TORONTO, NICE LOGO—A LEAF?
> —Sign for the visiting Maple Leafs

IT MAY BE SPRING, BUT THE LEAFS BLOW.
> —When the Leafs came to town on a los-
> ing streak

KNOCK, KNOCK—WHO'S THERE? SCOTTY BOWMAN!
> —After the Detroit coach accidentally
> locked himself in a room at the San Jose
> Arena

KASPARAITIS CAN BE CURED IN OUR LIFETIME.
> —A playful knock on the New York Is-
> landers' Darius Kasparaitis

Two More Good Signs

LA: POSITIVE STINKING.

> —Banner at the Great Western Forum,
> after the Kings closed out a season on a
> losing streak

PLAY DIRTY—AND WIN!

> —Banner in Boston Garden for the Big,
> Bad Bruins of the late sixties and seven-
> ties (The Bruins were tough customers
> but had trouble winning the big ones)

East vs. West

One of the great traditions of hockey is the rivalry between East and West. This is not an old-fashioned thing; the rivalry exists to-day. It was present in the 1994 Stanley Cup finals between the New York Rangers and the Vancouver Canucks. The Easterners had the glossy reputation and the big names; the Western team was bent on an upset. In the past, it's been the other way around. But whenever East meets West in hockey, there is an undeniable element of geographic animosity.

The tradition dates back to the earliest years of Stanley Cup play. "The champions swept the Easterners off their feet with dashing speed and relentless backchecking," wrote a breathless columnist for the *Vancouver Sun*, following the home team's victory over Ottawa in the 1915 Cup finals. "Vancouver clearly and cleanly fulfilled every claim to superiority over the Easterners," he concluded.

Ten years later it was the same story. "The Easterners are learning how hockey should be played from Western teams," crowed the *Victoria (B.C.) Colonist*. Victoria had just won its one and only Stanley Cup over a star-studded Montreal team—a vindication, said the paper, of Western-style hockey over the "effete East" (its term). Lester Patrick, who later became one of the founding fathers of New York Ranger hockey, coached those triumphant Victoria Cougars, and even he got caught up in the rivalry. "The Canadiens came west and those Easterners who came with them in their hard derby hats bet their last dollar that an upstart team in Victoria couldn't stop them," said Patrick many years later. "Who could stop Morenz and Joliat and Boucher? Who could score on the great Vezina? But I knew we'd win, because our second line would just tire them out, and it did." In the East players generally played all sixty minutes of a game; Patrick in the West had come up with the innovation of interchangeable lines. Patrick's team beat the greats from Montreal, and in so doing changed the game of hockey.

But Victoria's win proved to be something of a swan song not only for the hometown Cougars, but for Western hockey as well. "Western arrogance was to melt faster than natural ice in an unseasonable thaw," wrote hockey historian John Thompson. Montreal beat Victoria the next year, taking the Cup back home to the East and beginning a long, long drought for Western hockey fans. A Western team did not win another Stanley Cup for fifty-eight years, until Wayne Gretzky and the Edmonton Oilers—first deemed "wimps" by the Eastern media, if you'll recall—turned the trick in 1984.

RINKS

"Probably the shabbiest rink I ever worked was the old arena in Providence, Rhode Island. The dressing room was a filthy mess. The shower was old and only sprouted a trickle of water, and the floors, which were cold and cracked wooden racks, were always covered with a layer of slime."

> —Referee Bruce Hood, recalling a minor league rink

"Boston Garden is a zoo. The fans are maniacal and the rink is downright grubby. Without question it is the worst rink in the NHL. It's old and shabby, and always looks as if it could use another coat of paint and at least two more vacuum cleanings."

> —Brad Park, writing in the early seventies about the home of the Bruins

"They had to practice in this little rink there on the fifth floor, called Iceland. It was really no bigger than a puddle, maybe 120 feet long, no more than 60 feet wide. One end was egg shaped, and the boards were metal. How could you really practice there?"

> —John Halligan, former PR director of the New York Rangers, talking about the team's practice rink at the old Madison Square Garden

"I love playing there. Some guy once threw a trailer hitch at me. They're a different breed of fan, but that gets me going. I won't miss the cockroaches. I wonder how long it will take before they cross the street."

> —Shane Curla of Dallas Stars, saying good-bye to old Chicago Stadium, former home of the Blackhawks

Hockey Outdoors

Before the advent of air-conditioned arenas jam-packed with hawkers selling the latest NHL merchandise, hockey used to be played outdoors on natural ice rinks. You not only had to be hardy to *play* hockey, you had to be hardy to *watch* it. "We didn't have a hockey game at Montreal," said a disgusted Calgary coach after a downpour had turned the ice into slush. "It was an exhibition of water polo." Fans got mad when this happened, players got mad, and fights broke out—even more than the usual number. A February cloudburst turned one Montreal-Toronto game into the hockey equivalent of a mud-wrestling match. "The play-ers with their water-soaked boots and uniforms were in anything but an angelic mood," wrote a reporter, "and it took little to pro-voke retaliation." Nowadays, if such a thing happened, NHL teams would simply start selling umbrellas with their logos on them.

Hockey Town

Montreal *is* Hockey Town. Toronto, Chicago, New York, Edmon-ton, Boston—they love their hockey in these places, but not quite the way Montreal does. "Hockey in Montreal is different than in most cities. It's a religion," said Rocket Richard, who himself at-tained hockey sainthood while playing for the Canadiens. Hockey is to Montreal what golf is to St. Andrews, Scotland. "There is ab-solutely no city in the world of sport (not even Green Bay) that is so inseparable from its team as Montreal is to its Canadiens," noted Gerald Eskenazi, the writer. But it's not just tradition-minded journalists who speak of this; so do the players. "Every player knows that hockey is king in the province of Quebec, and a fierce pride seems to ooze out of every crack in the old build-ing," said Brad Park, describing the feeling of visiting players at the Forum. Park's time in the NHL was a generation ago, but to-day's players would probably say much the same thing.

The Montreal Canadiens are to hockey what the Celtics are to basketball, or the Yankees to baseball. They represent a storied history and a winning tradition. "We tried to upset a dynasty," said Derek Sanderson after his Bruins lost to the Canadiens in a Stanley Cup playoff series in the sixties. "And when you try to do that, you have to have luck. For some reason, the Canadiens al-ways seem to have the luck. So it must be more than luck, eh?" Yep, that's right. "It's like you're maneuvering in the shadow of a battleship," Don Cherry said years later while coaching a differ-ent Bruin team that nevertheless experienced the same results against Montreal. "You're always in the shadow of knowing how good they are." Babe Pratt, the defenseman turned scout, put it another way. When told that a young up-and-coming team had earned the right to play the powerhouse Canadiens in the playoffs, he said, "That's like busting your ass to be on the Titanic." Meaning: When you play the Canadiens, you're sunk.

A roll call of Montreal Canadiens contains some of the most storied names in the history of hockey: Rocket Richard, the Pocket Rocket, Guy LaFleur, Mahovlich, Dryden, Cournoyer, Beliveau, Boom Boom, Jacques Plante, Gump, Roy, Irvin, Blake, Bowman—the list goes on and on. It takes talent to win all those Stanley Cup championships, and the Canadiens certainly had that. Not only did opposing teams usually get beaten when they visited the Forum, they got beaten *the same way*. "The Canadiens' system hasn't changed much," said Henri Richard. "We try to get it out of our end as fast as we can." That they did, with unrivalled Gallic flair. "On the ice the Canadiens swoop and gambol, skating like fury and burning with zeal. They are somehow romantic, like Scaramouche or Cyrano," wrote Peter Gzowski after witnessing one Montreal team, vintage 1958, in action.

Montreal starts every season with one goal: to win the Stanley Cup. Achieving anything less is considered a failure. "In all the time I played for Montreal," said Ken Dryden, "I never once had the feeling that there was any other goal for the Montreal Canadiens than to win the Stanley Cup." The Canadiens have succeeded in that goal more than any other team, so much so that their fans have come to think of the Cup as something they own and rent out to other NHL teams from time to time. There is that great story of the Montreal fan who tried to steal the Cup after the Canadiens lost to Chicago in the 1961 playoffs. Upset that his team's string of consecutive Stanley Cup titles was stopping at five, he cracked the display case window, scooped up the grandest of all hockey treasures, and ran off. A cop caught him red-handed, though, and later the fan was brought before a judge to argue his case. "Your Honor," he said, "I was simply taking the Cup back to Montreal, where it belongs."

The Only Damn Thing That Needs to Be Said about the Lockout That Knocked Out Part of the 1994–1995 Season

"The hockey lockout has been settled. They've finally stopped bickering, and they can get down to some serious bloodshed."
—Conan O'Brien, comedian

12

SLAP SHOTS

Here's a roundup of some funny things that have been said about hockey over the years, including great lines about rotten teams, limp-wristed shooters, heavy-footed skaters, thickheaded players, the Stanley Cup, and some timeless hockey quotes.

GREAT LINES ABOUT BAD TEAMS

"Here's how bad the Islanders are: They've got Czechs defecting to get away from them."
—*The Sporting News*

"The Sharks are the only team in the NHL whose players have more teeth than wins."
—Ray Engan, comic

"The groundhog saw his shadow today. You know what that means in Ottawa? Six more weeks of losing."
—Disgruntled Ottawa fan

"The Mighty Ducks are laying goose eggs."
> —Reporter Robyn Norwood, during an
> Anaheim losing streak

"A winning streak for them was when they had back-to-back days off."
> —Joke about a poor Flyers team

"Someone tell the Sharks they have a game tonight, because they missed the last one."
> —Bud Geracie, sportswriter

GREAT LINES ABOUT SLOW-FOOTED SKATERS

"He's good, but he was the Slow-vak on the Slovak team in Lille-hammer."
> —Sportswriter Kevin Dupont, on Peter
> Stastny of the St. Louis Blues

"Sheppard skates slower than a tax refund."
> —Former coach, on Ray Sheppard of the
> Red Wings

"You skate like you're carrying a piano on your back. But do you have to stop and play it too?"
> —An oldie but goodie, about a slow skater

"I've got the only player in the league who can't skate."
> —Former Chicago coach Billy Reay, on
> defenseman Andre Lacroix

"I could have timed you with a calendar."
> —A coach, watching a young Brett Hull
> run a sprint

"We're so good defensively because we're so slow that none of our defensemen can get up the ice fast enough to be caught by the other team's offense."

> —Flyers coach Keith Allen, explaining why slow-footedness was a virtue on his team

A Famous Skinny Guy

"He's so skinny, he could fit in a McDonald's straw."

> —Writer on the young Wayne Gretzky

A Gloomy Gus

"I was in a bar and they asked Pulford to leave so they could start 'Happy Hour.'"

> —NHL executive, on glum-faced coach Bob Pulford

Cheapskates

"He's tighter than a buzzard's butt in a power dive."

> —Blake Hull, on his tight-cheeked brother, Brett

"He was so cheap he wouldn't give a worm to a blind bird."

> —Defenseman Babe Pratt, on his former boss, Lester Patrick of the New York Rangers

"Lester isn't close or tight, but he's adjacent."

> —Babe Pratt again, on Patrick

"He's so cheap, he wouldn't pay ten cents to see the Statue of Liberty take a swan dive into New York Harbor."
> —Conn Smythe, on old-time Blackhawk manager Bill Tobin

"Louie would reverse the charges on a ten-cent phone call."
> —Player, on old-time NHL defenseman Lou Fontinato

"He wouldn't give you a straw hat in a blizzard."
> —Comment on Weston Adams, Sr., one-time owner of Boston Bruins

Dumb Guys

"Bob Kelly was so dumb that his name was the only name that was written on the Stanley Cup in crayon."
> —Broadcaster Gene Hart, on former Flyer Bob Kelly

"If you put those four heads together, you've got a good start to a rock pile."
> —Mario Marois of St. Louis, seeing four thick-headed teammates skating together

Ugly Guys

"He had a face that looked like it had been kissed by the A Train."
> —Writer, on the busted-up pug of Terry O'Reilly

"He'd better get married soon because he's getting uglier every day."

> —Mark Recchi, on Flyers teammate Stewart Malgunas, who gets cut up and bruised a lot in hockey fights

BAD, BAD, BAD

The New York Islanders had just taken a terrible beating and a reporter, half in jest, asked their coach, Al Arbour, if he'd like to shoot his team. Arbour replied, "If I did, and I shot like my team, nobody would get hurt." Here are some good lines about bad shots, bad checkers, and bad stick handlers:

"Pierre Larouche couldn't check his hat."

> —Joke about former NHL player

"He couldn't shoot the puck into the ocean if he was standing on shore."

> —Classic line about a poor-shooting winger

"When the puck came to him it looked like it was alive and something to beat to death. Bang it! Cut it!"

> —Boston's Harry Sinden, on the way Philadelphia's Dave Schultz handled the puck

"Staszak faded faster than a tan in Toledo."

> —Sportswriter Brian McFarlane, about a junior phenom who couldn't stick, check, or pass in the NHL and fizzled as a pro

A GOOD CHECKING TEAM

"They were checking us so closely I could tell what brand of deodorant they were using."

> —Philly's Gary Dornhoefer, after playing Montreal

GREAT LINES BY OLD-TIME SPORTSWRITERS

"They harried the Ottawa forwards like a rat terrier landlord hounds his tenants."

> —Sportswriter Al Hardy, watching Vancouver handle Ottawa in a 1921 game

"Ottawa's defense held tighter than the warts on a golf ball."

> —Al Hardy again, on a tough Ottawa team

"For fifty minutes that lone tally was guarded as forcefully as the Royal Mint on Sussex Street."

> —Sportswriter Ed Barker, on a 1–0 lead by Ottawa that held up

"They clung to their slender lead like a bulldog to the seat of a tramp's trousers."

> —One more from Al Hardy, on the same game

"They have as much chance as a snowball in a Turkish bath."

> —Sportswriter, assessing Montreal's chances in a turn-of-the century game against Winnipeg

THOUGHTS ON STANLEY

"It's still quaint to hear a grown man wax passionate about winning a cup called Stanley. For whatever reason, the moniker 'Stanley' lacks a certain heroism, passion, a sense of glamour and mystery. Analogies would be calling the thing the Harry Cup or the Edgar Cup or the Marvin Cup."
—Lowell Cohn, sportswriter

"The Stanley Cup can look like a beautiful wedding cake, its bands of inscribed names cascading the length of the column that supports the bowl. A looser interpretation might be that it more closely resembles the gizmo that a local garage pulls under a car's crankcase for an oil change."
—Kevin Paul DuPont, sportswriter

UNRELATED FOOTBALL QUESTION, AND CHEAP LAWYER JOKE

"Now that San Francisco 49er quarterback Steve Young has his law degree, will he be playing for the San Jose Sharks?"
—Kit Miller, sports fan

USE THIS TOAST

If you ever find yourself introducing someone at a party or a banquet, you might think about trying this line used by a speaker who was introducing the hockey broadcaster Cactus Jack Wells at a gathering in his honor:

"Thank you for coming tonight. You know, a great many famous people have come to Jack's home over the years, and I see many of them in the audience tonight. But none of it has changed Jack; he's the same guy he's always been. He's just a guy who treats everyone the same, rich or poor, unknown or famous. He treats them all . . . shitty!"

HOCKEY CURMUDGEONS

Some people actually don't like hockey. So what are they doing in a hockey book? You're right. Trow da bums out!

"Hockey is the sport for the cerebrally challenged. How else does one describe a sport in which the genitals are always protected but it is optional to wear a helmet?"
                                    —James Christie, Toronto writer

"Hockey is basketball with no brains, one tooth, two halftimes and a thousand turnovers."
                                    —Dave Kindred, sportswriter

"I feel about hockey the way other columnists feel about basketball and Frisbee. I don't go out of my way to cover them."
                                    —Larry Merchant, columnist

"It would be a better game if it were played in mud."
                                    —Jimmy Cannon

CLASSIC HOCKEY LINES

If they had a place in the Hockey Hall of Fame for great lines, these utterances would be enshrined:

"If you can't beat 'em in an alley, you can't beat 'em on the ice."
                                    —Toronto owner Conn Smythe, uttering
                                      one of the most famous of all hockey
                                      maxims

"We're losing at home and we're losing on the road. My failure as a coach is I can't think of anywhere else to play."
                                    —Harry Neale, former hockey coach

"Take the shortest route to the puck—and arrive in ill humor."
> —Fred Shero's advice on how to play hockey

"Win together today and we'll walk together forever."
> —Coach Fred Shero, inspiring his team before a game

"He looked like Bobby Orr out there. Some nights, however, he looks like iron ore."
> —Coach Tom Webster, on defenseman Rob Blake

"You just keep shootin', and sometimes they go in and sometimes they don't."
> —Bill "Cowboy" Flett, on goal scoring

"Don't get the game confusing."
> —Toe Blake, hockey coach, on keeping things simple for players

"I feel eighteen. If we'd lost I'd feel dead."
> —Frank Mahovlich, age thirty-three, asked how he felt after Montreal's "miracle" Stanley Cup win over Boston in 1979

"Only my humility."
> —Boston sportswriter Tom Fitzgerald, after being asked "Do you have anything to declare?" by a customs officer as he returned to the U.S. following that 1979 Boston loss to Montreal in the Stanley Cup

A classic line about a classic hockey player: "Bobby Orr has sixteen variations of fast." Photo by Bruce Bennett

"Keep your stick on the ice and skate like hell."
　　　　　　　　　—Stan Mikita, on how to play the game

"He has sixteen variations of fast."
　　　　　　　　　—Classic line about the skating skills of
　　　　　　　　　the great Bobby Orr

"You hockey puck!"
　　　　　　　　　—Comedian Don Rickles's favorite insult

"Study the great ones."
　　　　　　　　　—Hockey scout Aldo Guidolin, giving
　　　　　　　　　advice to a youngster on how to succeed
　　　　　　　　　in hockey

Hockey Is . . .

"Canadians play hockey, talk hockey and dream hockey as naturally as they breathe. Hockey, better than any other thing, expresses Canada. It is perhaps our only truly national expression that cuts across language, race, age and distance."
                    —Bruce Hutchison, Canadian writer

"Hockey is murder on the ice."
                    —Jim Murray, sportswriter

"Hockey is a man's game. The team with the most men wins."
                    —Brian Burke, former hockey player

"Call them pros, call them mercenaries, but in fact they're just grown-up kids who've learned on the frozen creek or the flooded corner lot that hockey is the greatest thrill of all."
                    —Hall of Famer Lester Patrick, on NHL players

INDEX